"Dear Lord, Lest I keep my complacent way, I must remember somewhere out there a person died for me today. As long as there must be war, I ask and I must answer, was I worth dying for?"

—ELEANOR ROOSEVELT CARRIED
A COPY OF THIS PRAYER BY AN UNKNOWN
AUTHOR UNTIL THE DAY SHE DIED.

WHISTLE STOP Café MYSTERIES

Finished 8/24/24

WHISTLE STOP
Café
≡MYSTERIES≡

DOWN FORGET-ME-NOT LANE

LESLIE GOULD

Guideposts

Whistle Stop Café Mysteries is a trademark of Guideposts.

Published by Guideposts
100 Reserve Road, Suite E200
Danbury, CT 06810
Guideposts.org

Cover and interior design by Müllerhaus
Cover illustration by Greg Copeland at Illustration Online LLC.
Typeset by Aptara, Inc.

ISBN 978-1-961126-69-5 (hardcover)
ISBN 978-1-961126-70-1 (epub)

Printed and bound in the United States of America
10 9 8 7 6 5 4 3 2 1

DOWN FORGET-ME-NOT LANE

CHAPTER ONE

R eady?" Debbie Albright knelt beside Ray Zink's wheelchair. He turned toward her, his eyes misty under his dark-blue garrison cap fringed by his snow-white hair. Was he thinking of that day eighty years ago when he'd rushed onto Omaha Beach as a nineteen-year-old in June of 1944? Would the early Thursday afternoon ceremony be too much for this precious, nearly ninety-nine-year-old veteran and dear, dear friend?

The guests had already gathered outside the depot for the ceremony to honor Ray, but Debbie would make an excuse for him if needed. "Are you all right?" she whispered.

Ray squared his shoulders under the army dress jacket that hung loosely on his frail frame. "Absolutely. Let's go."

Debbie stood, stepped behind his chair, and then pushed Ray through the open doors of the depot, past pots of red and purple petunias, and out to the parking lot, where a podium, white tent, and chairs waited. Ray had been movie-star handsome as a young man, and it was still evident in his features. But it was his kind and humble disposition that drew people to him, and at least part of why the town was eager to honor him in this way.

The warm June sunshine welcomed them, along with newscaster Jonathon Bell. Debbie had invited him from Columbus. His cameraman, who wore jeans and a T-shirt, filmed as Jonathon said to Ray, "I'd like to interview you after the ceremony, if that's all right with you."

Ray gave him a thumbs-up. Debbie smiled and kept pushing the chair.

A hundred or more citizens of Dennison were already seated in the shade of the tent, along with Ray's younger sister, Gayle, and his niece, Trudy, who had also come from Columbus.

As Debbie wheeled Ray into the tent—decorated with red, white, and blue bunting and twinkle lights—the attendees rose to their feet. When Debbie stopped his chair at the front, everyone began to clap. Debbie's eyes filled with tears.

Greg Connor, chairman of the chamber of commerce and a good friend of Debbie's, stepped to the podium and faced Ray as the crowd stopped clapping and sat down. "Welcome, Ray." Greg's blue eyes seemed even more brilliant than usual as he met Ray's gaze. "Thank you for your service to our country eighty years ago and for your continued service to our town in the years since." Greg's grandfather had died in World War II, decades before Greg was born. He respected Ray all the more because of it.

Greg addressed the audience. "We're gathered here today to honor Ray Zink and also to remember the more than four hundred thousand American soldiers who died during World War II and the sixteen million who served during the war."

Debbie's heart swelled at Greg's words. She'd learned so much about World War II, both on the home front and in the war zones, since she'd moved back home to Dennison.

"First we'll hear from Kim Smith, curator of our museum," Greg said, "and then from Ray himself. And I just found out that we have a couple of special guests who've traveled here to honor Ray today also."

Debbie wondered who they could be. She'd helped plan the event and hadn't heard about any special guests. She positioned Ray's wheelchair in front of the podium, facing the audience, then sat near him in the first row of chairs as Kim stepped to the podium.

Kim talked about Dennison during World War II and the many young men of all races, ethnicities, and backgrounds who enlisted in the military or were drafted and then sent overseas. "Ray is the last remaining World War II veteran living in Dennison," she said, "which makes him our very own treasure. We don't take his service nor his long life for granted. Not only did he help liberate Europe from the Nazis and preserve the free world, but he's helped to preserve our own history ever since, while also assisting veterans who returned from Korea, Vietnam, the Gulf, Iraq, and Afghanistan."

Debbie didn't know that Ray had helped other veterans, but she wasn't surprised. He was one of the kindest and most generous people she had ever met.

Kim gave more information about Ray's service. He had landed on Omaha Beach during the D-Day and Normandy Campaign then made his way through northern France. He'd taken part in the beginning of the liberation of the Netherlands, where he'd been wounded and recovered in a hospital in England. Then he had been assigned to a unit that worked with the British Royal Engineers to clear land mines.

"He played a part in freeing the island of Guernsey in the Channel Islands and then was injured a second time in 1945. After recovering again in a British hospital, he returned home to the US." She went on to list his medals, including a Purple Heart and a Bronze Star.

Jonathon Bell's cameraman was off to the side, filming the speakers while Jonathon sat in an aisle chair, scrolling on his phone, which seemed odd to Debbie.

"We can never fully express our gratitude for everything you've done," Kim told Ray. "But we hope you feel appreciated. Now, as I understand it, you want to say a few words." She handed him the microphone.

He started by saying, "Thank you, Kim. I'm honored to be here today. Every morning, I wake up grateful for another day on this earth and in this town. I've been blessed beyond measure. I don't know why the Good Lord saw fit to save me twice during the war when so many never returned, but I haven't taken a minute of the last eighty years for granted. I want to be worthy of this life that the Lord has given me."

Debbie made eye contact with Gayle, who sat in the front row. Both women had to wipe away tears.

Ray went on to thank Greg, Kim, and Debbie for the ceremony, and then he honored the men he'd served with. "All of those who returned and all of those who didn't are always in my memories." He patted his chest. "And in my heart. Thank you again, everyone."

He passed the microphone to Greg while everyone applauded.

Greg announced, "Speaking of the men Ray served with, we have Ohio State Representative Heather Clark here today." Ray stirred as Greg continued. "She's the daughter of Representative Leland Clark, who passed away nine years ago. He served with Ray in Holland

and on Guernsey." He gestured toward the back of the crowd. "Representative Clark, please come forward."

A woman who wore a navy pencil skirt and matching jacket started down the middle aisle with a leather bag over her shoulder. She appeared to be in her late fifties or early sixties and wore her auburn hair shoulder-length. She was followed by a young woman who seemed to be in her late teens, with straight red hair falling over one side of her face.

Heather Clark beamed at Ray and then accepted the microphone from Greg. "Thank you, Mr. Connor, for your kindness in having us here today." She put an arm around the young woman. "This is my niece, Ruby Clark, who is also here to honor Ray Zink."

Ruby gave a shy wave before her aunt continued.

"My father talked about Ray Zink a lot, because he was Ray's sergeant," Heather said. "When I found out that Ray was being honored today, I knew Ruby and I had to come." She took a picture frame out of her bag and held it up. "This sat on my father's desk until the day he died. It's a photo of him with Ray on Guernsey in June of 1945. They both look so full of hope and determination in spite of everything they'd already seen and been through." She turned to Ray. "I've made copies of the photo for myself and Ruby. I want you to have this one."

Heather gave the microphone back to Greg and approached Ray.

Ray took the photo in one hand and Heather's free hand in the other. "Thank you," he said, his voice trembling with emotion. "Thank you for this picture and for coming. I remember Leland with fondness. I hope you can stay for the reception."

"I wouldn't miss it," Heather assured him. "I hope we'll have time to chat."

Ray let go of Heather's hand and beckoned to Ruby. She stepped to his side and took his hand.

"I'm pleased to meet you, Ruby," Ray told her. "Thank you for coming."

She gave him a small smile, ducking her head so that her long hair swung forward to hide more of her face.

"We'll see you at the reception," Heather said.

The audience clapped, and Heather and Ruby started toward the back, where a young man in a black suit stood.

"Thank you, Representative Clark and Ruby. What a nice surprise to have you here today," Greg said. "We have one more surprise for you, Ray. Oliver Godfrey has come all the way from Guernsey to honor you."

The crowd murmured in surprise.

Ray turned to Debbie with wide eyes. "What's happening? Should I know that name?"

"I'm not sure," she answered.

A short, thin man in corduroy pants and a brown plaid jacket made his way toward Greg. He had gray hair and appeared to be in his midsixties or so. A leather satchel was strapped across his chest.

"Oliver has been searching for Ray for the last decade and finally tracked him down a month ago. When he found out we were having a ceremony today to honor Ray, he traveled all this way to be here." Greg handed Oliver the microphone.

The man seemed overwhelmed for a moment but then turned to Ray and said, "My mother was Adele Martin, the little girl you saved in June of 1945. I can't believe I've finally found you."

The crowd gasped. Ray reached for Debbie and she took his hand, her own shaking as much as his.

"My mother was ten years old," Oliver continued. "Her father had been in the service since 1939, and he was scheduled to arrive in St. Peter Port that day. Her grandmother was ill, so she was delayed getting down to the docks. She took a shortcut and began running through a field toward the road, but—unknown to her—a live mine was in that field. Ray Zink risked his own life to save hers, injuring himself in the process." Oliver paused a moment and then said, "I grew up hearing stories about Ray Zink. My mother owed her life to him, and so do I. He's a true American hero."

The crowd sat in shocked silence for a moment. But then Greg began to clap, and others did too. Soon the entire audience was standing, clapping, and cheering. And Debbie wiped tears from her eyes once again.

The ceremony wasn't what she'd planned—but it couldn't have been better. And Ray deserved every second of it.

Half an hour later, Ray sat in the lobby of the depot as the last of the crowd filed by to shake his hand and then enjoy cookies made by Janet Shaw, who co-owned the Whistle Stop Café with Debbie. Tables were set up in the lobby, and more people than usual were squeezed into the café. The museum was open, and part of the crowd drifted that way.

Once everyone had greeted Ray, Jonathon Bell interviewed him, asking a few follow-up questions about what Ray had said during the celebration.

After he finished the interview, Jonathon said, "I'm fascinated by World War II memorabilia and have been collecting it for years."

"What made you interested in it?" Ray asked.

"I have a great-uncle who served. He didn't have children, so I inherited his uniform twenty years ago when he passed away. After that, I bought more World War II items at estate sales and that sort of thing. Now I buy things online." He held up his phone. "In fact, I bid on a jacket a few minutes ago." Before Ray could respond, Jonathon shook his hand. "Thanks for your time, as well as for your service. I'm going to go walk through the museum and then leave. We have to get back to Columbus to film a high school graduation. Five generations in one family have graduated from the same school."

"Nice," Debbie said. "Thank you again."

Jonathon gave her a nod.

Debbie pushed Ray's chair to the table where Gayle sat with Trudy, and grabbed a cup of coffee and a cookie for him.

Then Debbie went into the café to check on Janet to see if she needed any help. "I've got this under control," Janet said from behind the counter where she was making a mocha. "Go mingle."

Debbie headed toward Ray's table but stopped to talk to Greg first. "When did you find out that Heather Clark and Oliver Godfrey were here?"

"Not until right before the ceremony began. Otherwise, I would have told you. Heather and her assistant found me about ten minutes before. They'd left a message at the chamber, but I missed it."

Debbie nodded at the young man in the suit who stood with Heather and Ruby. "Is that her assistant?"

"Yes," Greg said. "He's a recent college graduate. He's working for a year before he goes to law school. And then Oliver arrived a few minutes before we started."

Where was Oliver? Debbie glanced around the lobby and found him talking with her parents. No doubt they had approached him. They always formed a welcome wagon.

"Oliver's arrival really shocked me," Greg said. "It's one thing to have the daughter of someone Ray served with come in from Columbus. But to have Oliver come all the way from the United Kingdom—that's nothing short of fantastic."

"Ray was obviously touched," Debbie said. "It's hard for me to picture someone running across a field of land mines to save a little girl. But it's completely in line with who Ray is, so if I could see anyone doing that, it would be him."

Greg shuddered. "I can't imagine being in that situation. And the closer my boys get to the age Ray was when he enlisted, the more real it all seems." Jaxon and Julian were in their midteens, and Ray had been newly eighteen when he'd been sent overseas.

Heather and Ruby approached Ray's table. Debbie excused herself to Greg and met them there, introducing them to Gayle and Trudy.

"How lovely that you were able to come," Gayle said to the representative. "We live in your district, but I had no idea your father served with my brother. What a special connection."

Heather smiled. "I can't tell you how much I wish I'd known Ray was in Ohio. Dad would have loved to reconnect. To think they were so close but never saw each other again." She shook her head. "It's such a shame."

"How did you find out about the celebration?" Debbie asked Heather.

"Last night on the news, when Jonathon mentioned that he was coming here today." Obviously, Heather was on a first-name basis with the newscaster. "He mentioned that Ray Zink landed on Omaha Beach, was injured in Holland, and cleared mines in the Channel Islands. That was Dad's exact route. I had a hunch they must have served together, and Jonathon confirmed it this morning when he texted me a photo of Ray as a soldier. It was the same young man in Dad's photo. Ruby and I packed up and hit the road—and my assistant, Graham, was able to join us here."

"Wonderful," Debbie said. "I'm so glad you were able to make it on such short notice."

"I'm really missing Dad today, but this is helping." Heather gestured to the medals on Ray's jacket. "One thing I don't understand is why Dad never got a Purple Heart. Weren't all soldiers who were injured in action by the enemy supposed to receive one?"

"That's right, as long as they required treatment by a medical officer at the time of the injury," Ray said. "But there were all sorts of paperwork snags. When it hadn't come through after several months, Leland said he'd petition the army to award him one after the war."

"He said it never arrived."

"Oh, that's too bad. It would be nice for you to have it now, to remember your father and Ruby's grandfather."

Ruby blushed. She really was a shy one.

Out of the corner of her eye, Debbie spotted Oliver Godfrey shaking her mom's hand and then her dad's before making his way toward Ray's table. When he reached them, Debbie introduced herself to Oliver and then introduced him to Heather and her group.

"Pleased to meet you," Heather said. "Dad always told us he'd rescued a little girl from a minefield on Guernsey. Were there two girls who were rescued?"

"I've never heard of another rescue like my mother's, but that doesn't mean there wasn't one. I do have some questions for Ray though."

"Go ahead," Ray replied.

"How did you manage to cross the field without setting off any mines?"

"It was the last mine in the field," Ray said. "The engineers had partly dismantled it and then stopped for lunch."

Heather crossed her arms. "I'm sure it was Dad who rescued the girl. I heard the story my entire life."

A chatting passerby bumped into Ray's chair. Ray jerked, and his coffee spilled onto his military jacket, including his medals. "Oh dear," he said. "Look what I've done."

Debbie grabbed a napkin and began dabbing at the coffee as Carl Miller, who was buying the dry-cleaning business in town from his older brother, paused at her side. "Let me take that to the shop. I'll clean it right away and have it back to you by morning."

Jonathon, Heather, and Oliver all watched as Debbie helped Ray remove his jacket. The cameraman stood behind Jonathon with the camera still on his shoulder.

Carl accepted the jacket from Debbie. "Stop by first thing in the morning. This will be ready by then."

"I will," she answered. "Thank you."

Carl nodded and hurried away.

Ray sighed. "I think I should go home and rest. This has all been wonderful, but I'm tired."

Trudy stood and helped her mother rise. "We'll give you a ride back to Good Shepherd, Uncle Ray."

"Will we see you again?" Heather asked him.

"You're welcome to join me at the retirement center for dinner." Ray shifted his gaze to Oliver. "You too, Mr. Godfrey. I'd love to chat with both of you more. Dinner starts at five. We're having meatballs and gravy, with apple pie for dessert."

"We'll be there," Heather said.

"So will I." Oliver smiled.

"Would you come for dinner too?" Ray asked Debbie as Trudy stepped behind his chair. "And invite Janet and Ian—I think Ian and Oliver might hit it off." Ian had emigrated from Scotland as a boy.

"Absolutely." She smiled down at him as he patted her hand.

Trudy pushed him to the exit with Gayle walking beside them. Ahead of them, Carl stepped out of the depot and turned toward his shop downtown, carrying Ray's jacket over his arm.

Debbie turned back to look at their surprise guests. When she saw the pinched expression on Heather's face, she gave Ray Zink credit for not only being kind and generous. He was also smart. She was willing to bet that Ian being from Scotland wasn't the only reason he'd asked for their presence at dinner.

CHAPTER TWO

When Debbie arrived at Good Shepherd, Oliver Godfrey was trying to pay for his meal in the lobby. But it was already paid for.

"Ray covered the cost," Ashley, the receptionist, explained. "He insisted."

"How very kind of him." Oliver slid his wallet into his back pocket. He turned and smiled at Debbie. "Miss Albright. How nice to see you again. I'm guessing the dining hall is across the lobby."

"Yes." Debbie pointed to the double doors. "Ray probably already has a table." She stepped up to the counter and opened her purse.

"Ray paid for you too," Ashley whispered.

"That stinker."

Ashley laughed. "Isn't he, though? The worst."

"The very worst." Debbie smiled. "It's his big day, and he pays for his guests."

"How dare he?" Ashley said.

"Exactly." Debbie closed her purse, thanked Ashley, and then followed Oliver toward the double doors.

"Ray usually sits over on the left side," she told Oliver.

Sure enough, there was Ray in his wheelchair. Kim's mother, Eileen Palmer, sat next to him, with Janet and her husband, Police

Chief Ian Shaw, across the table. Heather, Ruby, and Graham hadn't arrived yet. The table would certainly be full.

Debbie led the way, patting Ray's shoulder in greeting as she reached the table. Then she wrapped an arm around Eileen, who had been the Dennison stationmaster during World War II and lived at Good Shepherd Retirement Center.

"We missed you today," Debbie said as she released Eileen.

"I'm sorry I wasn't there," Eileen said. "I've been having hip pain and not moving very fast or far as of late."

"How awful. I'm sorry to hear that."

"It's all right, dear. It's just a part of getting older," Eileen replied.

Janet stood and hugged Debbie, followed by Ian. Debbie introduced both to Oliver.

"Good to meet you," Ian said in his slight Scottish brogue.

Oliver beamed. "Good to meet you, mate. Where in Scotland are you from?"

"Ach, you have a good ear. I barely have an accent anymore with all the years I've lived here."

"Definitely Scottish. I'm guessing the south."

Ian nodded. "I take it you haven't spent your entire life on Guernsey."

"You're right," Oliver said. "I've spent time near London and in Scotland. Beautiful country." He turned his attention to Ray. "Of course, Ohio is beautiful too."

Ray chuckled. "I love Ohio and the US, but there's beauty around the world. And I'm a little partial to the UK. I recovered there twice, cared for by American, English, and Scottish hospital staff."

"Where?" Oliver asked.

"The North Somerset village of Wraxall for my first recovery," Ray replied. "Southampton for my second."

"Ah, Southampton," Oliver said. "I've taken the ferry from there to Guernsey more times than I can count."

"I also served in Cornwall."

Oliver's eyes grew wide. "You certainly saw a lot of England."

"I did," Ray said. "But I never made it to London. They didn't need visitors when I was in that area. Still, I would like to have seen it."

"I'm rather fond of London," Oliver said. "I lived there when I was a young man, after I first left Guernsey."

The server came, and Debbie explained that they expected three more guests. The young woman took their drink orders then hurried away.

"Mr. Zink, I would love to hear about your memories of Guernsey," Oliver said.

"Guernsey was both beautiful and terrifying," Ray said. "The inhabitants had to live under a five-year occupation by the Nazis, who set land mines all over, and that was more than anyone should have to face. There were so many atrocities." His voice trailed off.

Debbie laid a hand on his arm. "Ray? You don't have to talk about it if you don't want to."

Ray shook off whatever he'd been remembering. "No, it's important to remember the horrors so we don't forget the lessons that came with them. Anyway, the Nazis left peacefully. Many were taken away to POW camps, and some were ordered to rebuild Europe. A few engineers were retained to help with the treacherous work of dismantling the mines left behind. It was amazing that there weren't more civilian casualties." A worried expression passed over his face. Despite his heroic words, the memories seemed difficult.

Oliver must have thought the same. "You, your fellow soldiers, and the Royal Engineers will always be heroes to those of us who hail from Guernsey. You saved countless lives."

Before Ray could respond, a voice sang out, "Sorry we're late!" Heather had arrived, with Ruby behind her.

Debbie stood and greeted the two of them. Then she asked, "Where's Graham?"

"He had plans back in Columbus," Heather answered. "I told him to go ahead. We drove separate cars."

The conversation shifted to lighter topics for the next few minutes as the drinks were served and the remaining orders taken. When the food arrived, Ian led the group in a prayer.

Then, as they all began eating, Heather said, "I hesitate to bring this up again, but I'd really like to figure out—"

Debbie braced herself for another claim that Heather's father had rescued Adele Martin rather than Ray.

But Heather surprised her by finishing with, "—any options we might have regarding Dad's missing Purple Heart. Do you have any ideas, Mr. Zink?"

"I've been thinking about that since you brought it up at the depot," Ray said. "I know there were often mistakes made in the paperwork. Do you know if your dad tracked down what happened? It seems to me that as a state representative, it would have been easy for him to do."

Heather pursed her lips. "I have no idea if he did or not. All I know is that he never received it."

"I believe you can still apply," Ray said. "It can be awarded posthumously."

"Really?" Heather's face brightened, and she patted Ruby's arm. "You may end up with Grandpa's Purple Heart after all."

Perhaps the others sensed that Ray was tired, because the conversation didn't return to Guernsey nor to Leland Clark's lack of a Purple Heart. Thankfully, Heather didn't bring up her theory that her father had rescued Adele Martin again.

As they finished eating, Debbie pulled up the six o'clock Columbus news on her phone and held it up for everyone to see. "I'm recording it at home," she said. "But I thought we could watch it now."

After the headlines, Ray's story, narrated by Jonathon, was the first feature. It showed clips from the ceremony and the interview with Ray. Jonathon wrapped it up by saying, "Ray Zink is our own Ohioan hero. We wish him the best this month as he celebrates eighty years since the Allies stormed Normandy and his ninety-ninth year of life."

Ray's party around the table clapped.

"That was wonderful," Heather said as the applause died down. "What an honor to share all of this with you."

Everyone agreed. The dinner had gone much better than Debbie had thought it would.

Heather and Ruby left right after dinner, before the apple pie, saying they wanted to get back to Columbus before it got too late.

On the other hand, Oliver stayed through the last bite, chatting with everyone. He was a skilled conversationalist, drawing out Ray, along with Eileen and Janet and Ian. He focused on Dennison, asking about the history of the town and the railroad.

When Eileen told him about the millions of troops passing through on the trains during World War II, he shook his head in disbelief. "Your country is so big," he said. "Growing up on Guernsey, it's hard to imagine such a vast, open space. Flying into Columbus and driving down here was an experience in itself, and yet I know it's such a small piece of your country."

"My parents can't get over the vastness of America either," Ian said. "Scotland is about the size of South Carolina. There's no comparing it to the United States."

"I don't know what Guernsey compares to," Oliver said. "It's only twenty-four square miles."

"And every inch of it is beautiful," Ray said.

"What was it like to grow up on a small island like that?" Janet asked.

"Like anywhere else, there was good and bad. You knew everyone's business, which wasn't always good. But people helped each other out, which was always good," Oliver said.

"Do you live there now?" Ian asked.

"No. I live in London." Oliver smiled. "I miss Guernsey. None of my family lives there anymore, so I don't get back much. I should change that."

Ray yawned, quickly covering his mouth.

Eileen said, "We should probably call it a night."

They all agreed. It had been a big day, and Debbie was ready to get home.

As everyone got up from the table, Oliver made his way to Ray's side. "Would it be all right if I stopped by in the morning, perhaps around ten? There are still a few questions I'd like to ask you, but I don't want to wear out my welcome."

"I'd like that," Ray told him. "Check in at the desk, and the receptionist will call me. I'll meet you in the lobby."

"Thank you. I'll see you in the morning." The words were barely out of Oliver's mouth when his phone dinged. He took it from his jacket pocket, read the screen, smiled, and then gave them a wave. "So good to spend time with all of you. Thank you for including me." Then he hurried toward the lobby, his phone still in his hand.

Debbie pushed Ray back to his room, with Eileen walking beside them to her own room. She said good night to both of them then headed home.

All the talk about Purple Hearts shifted her thoughts to Reed, her fiancé who had been killed in Afghanistan twenty years before. Time—and the Lord—had helped comfort her in her grief, but she still thought about Reed frequently. He'd been awarded a posthumous Purple Heart. His mother, Betsy, had offered it to Debbie, who had insisted that Betsy keep it. It felt right for the medal to stay with his mother.

As she reached her Craftsman-style home—which she'd bought from Ray—her phone dinged with a text from Greg. HOME FROM THE GAME. Both of his sons played summer basketball, and the older one, Jaxon, had a game at the high school. THE BOYS ARE EATING PIZZA AND WATCHING A MOVIE. WANT TO GO FOR A WALK?

I'D LOVE THAT, Debbie texted back. JUST GOT HOME. GIVE ME A FEW MINUTES.

Her heart skipped a beat. She and Greg had started dating—a movie, a casual dinner, a couple of hikes—over the past few weeks after spending a year getting to know each other. An evening walk with him sounded even better than relaxing by herself on her couch.

She put on her walking shoes and went out to the porch to wait, breathing in the honeysuckle in bloom on the trellis along the side of the house. The lowering sun brought a chill to the early June day, and Debbie stepped back into the house for a light sweater. By the time she returned to the porch, Greg was coming up the steps.

He smiled at her. "How was dinner?"

"Better than I expected, actually," Debbie said. "Heather Clark mentioned her father's missing Purple Heart but didn't drill Ray about who rescued Adele Martin again."

"Good. That was a little weird."

Debbie nodded in agreement.

Greg zipped his sweatshirt. "Did I ever tell you I have my grandfather's Purple Heart?"

"No." Debbie led the way to the sidewalk. "Tell me about it."

"It's in a shadow box in my dresser." He shrugged. "I should put it on the mantel or something, huh?"

"Why haven't you?" They turned onto the sidewalk and headed toward the depot.

"When I see it, it makes me sad to think about all my dad lost. Mom's the one who put it in a shadow box. I guess I've learned to associate it with grief rather than pride."

"What do Jaxon and Julian think of it?"

"I don't think they've seen it before. I need to show them. They enjoyed Ray's ceremony today. Right now they're watching *The Great Escape*."

Debbie asked, "That's a classic, right?"

"Right. My dad wasn't one for World War II movies, but I couldn't get enough of them growing up. I imagined my grandfather in every one I saw. I don't think Julian and Jaxon do that though. I think they're just interested in World War II in general."

"Do you have anything else of your grandfather's, like his uniform or other medals?"

Greg shook his head. "I have no idea what happened to his things. I don't know if Grandma kept them or if she ever even received them."

"What was your grandfather's name?"

"Earl Gregory Connor Sr.," Greg answered. "Dad was named after him. And I was too, obviously."

"Where was he killed?"

"In northern Africa," Greg said. "His body was never brought back to the States. My grandmother was always sad about that."

They started walking again, heading toward the park. Debbie intertwined her fingers with Greg's, wishing there was a way she could help him bring some closure to the past. Her thoughts went to the other questions that had been raised at supper. Why hadn't Leland Clark received his Purple Heart? And why did his daughter believe he'd rescued Oliver's mother?

Early the next morning Debbie headed toward the Whistle Stop Café, looking forward to a normal Friday without any event planning. Her phone rang, and she dug it from her purse, alarmed. No one called her at seven a.m., not even her mother. *Dennison Dry Cleaners* appeared on the screen. Relieved, she answered the call.

"Hello, Carl." She began crossing the street.

"Debbie?" He sounded frantic.

The hair stood up on the back of her neck. "What's the matter?"

"Ray's jacket is gone."

She couldn't have heard him correctly. "What do you mean?"

"I just came into work. It was hanging up when I left last night, clean and ready for you to pick up this morning. But it's not there now. I've searched everywhere that I might have left it."

Debbie froze in the middle of the street. "Was the door locked?"

"Yes. And the security system was set when I unlocked the door this morning."

A horn honked, and Debbie jerked her head up to find Greg stopped in his pickup. She waved and hurried toward him.

He rolled down his window. "Everything all right?"

"Every*one* is all right," she replied, holding the phone away from her face. She didn't want him to think someone had been injured or was ill. Or worse. "I'll send you a text about what's going on."

"Okay, but please do it from the sidewalk. Take care." He rolled up his window and continued on his way.

Debbie returned to her call. "Carl, I'll be there soon. I'll contact Ian Shaw and let him know what happened."

"Thank you, Debbie." Relief was clear in his tone.

"I'm just a few minutes away. Sit tight. We'll get this worked out."

She ended the call and then immediately rang Ian as she started to backtrack to her house. She needed to take her car to save time.

Ian answered at once. "Debbie? It's pretty early. Is everything all right?"

"Not really." She explained the situation. "Can you meet me at the dry cleaners?"

"I'll be right there."

Next Debbie called Janet. "I'm so sorry, but I'll be late. Ray's jacket has gone missing from the dry cleaners."

"I'll call Paulette and see if she can come in ASAP instead of at nine," Janet answered. Paulette was Greg's mother who worked part-time at the café. "In the meantime, I'll manage. Call Ian if you haven't yet."

"Thanks. I just got off the phone with him. I hope we find the jacket right away."

"Me too," Janet said.

Surely it had simply been misplaced. Who would be so cruel as to steal a uniform jacket from a World War II veteran?

CHAPTER THREE

When she arrived at the dry cleaners, Ian was already there, with a backpack slung over his shoulder. Together, they walked up to the front door. Ian tried the door and then knocked. When Carl didn't appear, he pulled out his phone and called him.

After a moment Ian said, "Carl, this is Ian Shaw. We're at the front door."

Carl unlocked and opened the door a minute later. "Come on in," he said. "I haven't touched anything." He stepped back to let them in. "The front door was locked and secure when I arrived, and so were the back door and the drive-through window. I don't know how anyone could have gotten inside without going through one of those." Carl led the way around the counter.

"Have you searched everywhere?" Ian asked. "In all the closets and cabinets? That sort of thing?"

"I've only checked in places I might have left it after cleaning it," Carl said. "Do you think someone would break in and hide it?"

"Not necessarily," Ian said. "But we need to establish that it's not on the premises. Let's take a look."

"Okay." Carl indicated the clothes on a circular rack, all pressed, hung, and ready to be returned to customers. "The jacket was hanging here. I had it separate from the other clothes because Debbie was going to pick it up this morning."

It took Debbie no time to confirm that the jacket was indeed not hanging on the rack.

Carl moved to a bank of cabinets on the far wall, on the other side of the cleaning machines. "I keep supplies over here." One by one, he opened the cabinets. Inside were jugs of fluids, cleaning tools, and business supplies.

They easily verified that the jacket wasn't in any of them.

He pointed to a tall cabinet along the far wall, past the pressing area. "I keep brooms, mops, and a bucket over there." He opened the door, revealing exactly that. There was no jacket in the cabinet.

He took them to the drive-through counter and then the shop counter. One by one he pulled out each drawer, although Debbie was confident that, even folded, the jacket wouldn't have fit in any of them. They were filled with pens, receipt books, rubber bands, wire hangers, and plastic bags.

When Carl closed the last drawer, Ian asked, "Who else has a key?"

"My brother, Elwood, who's selling the place to me."

Ian made a note then asked, "Any security footage?"

Carl gestured toward the back of the room where there was a desk that held a computer. "I was going through it, but I haven't seen anything."

Ian asked, "Mind if I look for myself?"

"Please do." Carl led the way to the desk. "I have cameras on both doors and the window."

The drive-through window was to the right, and a long rack spanned the entire length of the room to the left. Ahead, at the end of the room and to the left, between the desk and the rack, was the back door.

Debbie examined the drive-through window while Ian stood at the desk watching the security footage.

"There's a photo of a raccoon who triggered the motion sensor on the camera at the back door. They come around to check out the dumpster in the alley. Besides that, nothing else triggered the cameras."

"Any other openings into the interior of the building?"

"No," Carl said. "Like I said, there's just the two doors and the drive-through."

Debbie pointed to a window high on the wall. "What about that?"

"It's a ventilation window from years ago," Carl said. "We have a better system now."

Debbie squinted against the morning light coming through the window. "It's a short drop from the window to the cabinet underneath," she said.

Ian squinted too. "And it appears to be unlatched."

"Really?" Carl stepped closer.

"Do you remember if it was latched yesterday?" Ian asked.

"I didn't notice," Carl said, his voice rising with anxiety. "For all I know it's been unlatched for months. I've never paid any attention to it."

"What's outside the window?"

Carl tilted his head. "A tree, but I'm not sure how close it is to the building."

Ian pointed to the space between the cabinet and the back door. "Was that jug on the floor yesterday?"

"I don't think so. It's window cleaner—it was on top of the cabinet," Carl answered, taking a step toward it.

"Don't touch it," Ian said.

Carl stopped. "Oh yeah. Sorry."

"It's all right. Let's take a look outside." Ian started for the back door.

Debbie and Carl followed him. The space between the building and the alleyway consisted of a graveled area with a dumpster, two parking spaces, and a small lawn with a picnic table under a tree. The top branches of the tree were mere inches from the window, which had a ledge, and the bottom branches were fairly high. Maybe someone could stand on the picnic table and swing up to the lower branch and then to the one nearest the ventilation window. Maybe.

"I have lunch out here on nice days," Carl said.

They'd reached the grassy area, which had a few sprinkler heads sticking out of it. Debbie scanned a muddy area around the base of the tree and then pointed to the picnic table. "Is that a footprint?" It was across three boards at the end of the table and faint, but it appeared to be from the bottom of some kind of athletic shoe.

Ian took a step closer. "Yes. Good eye, Debbie. Carl, are the sprinklers automatic?"

Carl nodded. "They're along the flower beds, out here and in the front," he said. "They were put in last fall."

"When do they run?"

"Tuesday, Thursday, and Saturday at nine p.m. for ten minutes."

"So last night?" Ian said.

"Right," Carl said. Debbie realized that would have been after the dinner at Good Shepherd with Ray.

"What time did you leave here yesterday?" Ian asked.

"Seven thirty," Carl answered. "Elwood and I left at the same time."

Ian took his camera and a ruler from the bag. He laid the ruler beside the shoe print then snapped a photo. The print was too faint for Debbie to make out exactly how long it was.

Ian stared up at the window. "If a thief got through that window, it would have to be someone fairly small, in good shape, and nimble."

"True," Debbie said. "But don't discount that someone else might have put a small, in shape, and nimble person up to the deed."

Ian sighed. "That's true too. In any case, at least we have a place to start."

Debbie folded her arms over her chest. "At the risk of gossiping, I may be able to give you a few names to add to that start."

Debbie sat in her car outside Dennison Dry Cleaners and called Janet. After she explained what was going on, she asked, "Mind if I go by Ray's and tell him what happened? I'd rather he heard the news in person from a friend."

"No problem," Janet answered. "Paulette is here, and it's relatively calm."

"Great. I won't be long."

After she hung up, she texted Greg. I'M ON MY WAY TO GOOD SHEPHERD TO TELL RAY THAT HIS JACKET IS MISSING FROM THE DRY CLEANERS. TALK TO YOU SOON.

Debbie slid her phone into her purse and then drove to the retirement center. Ray was an early riser, but after the excitement of the day before, she knew he might have slept in. If he wasn't up yet, she wouldn't wake him. She'd wait and come back after the lunch rush.

But when she hurried through the double doors of Good Shepherd, she spotted Ray in the lobby. She guessed he was waiting for the dining hall to open at eight for breakfast.

Ray spotted her and put his hands on the wheels of his chair. "Debbie, what are you doing here so early? Is everything all right?"

"I need to talk to you about your army jacket," Debbie answered, her stomach rolling with nerves. She dreaded telling the sweet man her news. "I just came from Dennison Dry Cleaners."

Ray leaned back in his chair. "Thank goodness. I thought there had been a tragedy or something. Was there a dry-cleaning accident?"

"No." Debbie sat down in a chair beside him. "Your jacket is missing. There's a possibility that it was stolen."

"Missing?" Ray echoed, his eyes wide. "Stolen?"

"We're not sure," Debbie said. "But Ian is on the case and has already been to the dry cleaners. Carl feels horrible. There's an unlocked ventilation window that someone may have accessed to get into the building."

"Who would steal my jacket?"

"It must have been someone who saw it yesterday and knew Carl took it to be cleaned."

Ray gripped the wheels of his chair. "I'm dumbfounded."

"We'll get it back," Debbie said firmly.

Ray didn't respond.

Debbie touched his arm. "What are you thinking?"

"I'm realizing that I haven't thought about what will happen to my uniform when I'm gone." He met her gaze. "I don't think it's something Trudy would want. Do you think Kim already has a collection of World War II uniforms?"

"You could ask her," Debbie said. "You might be surprised."

He didn't respond at first. After a moment he said, "It's a shame that Leland Clark never got his Purple Heart when he has family to leave it to. Heather said they don't have any of his uniforms either."

"I didn't hear that," Debbie said.

"You were in the café," Ray said. "I haven't thought about Leland in years. Now I can't seem to stop thinking about him. I spent more time with him than anyone else during the war. Normandy. Through France and Belgium. Then in the Netherlands. In Cornwall and on Guernsey. We went through a lot together."

"And yet you never saw each other once you returned?"

"That's right," Ray said. "I didn't tell Heather this, but I wrote to him after he was elected to the statehouse. I had read in the Columbus paper about him being elected and wanted to reconnect, but I never received a reply. One time when I was in Columbus visiting Gayle, I called his office and left a message inviting him to meet up, but I didn't hear back from him that time either. After that, I didn't try to contact him again. I thought maybe I'd gotten the wrong Leland Clark. Or that he didn't want to associate with me because I reminded him of the war."

"What do you remember about him?" Debbie asked.

"He was from Kentucky originally. He'd had three years of college before the war, and his goal was to go to Harvard Law School after. I forgot to ask Heather if that worked out for him. It seems as though some law school did." Ray sighed. "Our lives here were so different, and yet in a foxhole, they say we're all the same. That was certainly true for the two of us."

"Would you like to see Heather again? Ask her more questions?"

"I don't know if that's necessary." He smiled. "From what I remember about Leland and observed about her yesterday, Heather takes after her father—gregarious and in charge. Ruby, on the other hand—not so much," Ray said. "I think the girl could use some encouragement."

Debbie felt the same way. But she couldn't tell whether either personality would be more likely to take an irreplaceable jacket.

CHAPTER FOUR

W hen Debbie arrived back at the café, a few of the tables were occupied. Harry Franklin and his granddaughter Patricia sat at their regular table, with Harry's dog, Crosby, at his feet. It was nice to have something appear normal.

"Good morning." Debbie smiled her brightest, hoping to put her worries aside for a while and focus on work.

Patricia held her cup in both hands. "Any news on Ray's jacket?"

Surprised, Debbie asked, "Did Janet tell you it's missing?"

Patricia shook her head. "Carl came in and got a cup of coffee. He said Ray's jacket was stolen. He's so upset about it that he got his brother to watch the shop so he could go for a walk."

"He said you stopped by the dry cleaners this morning," Harry added.

"Yes. That's right," Debbie replied.

Harry reached down and patted Crosby. "Did someone really steal Ray's jacket?"

"It's a possibility," Debbie answered. "All we know for sure right now is that it's missing."

Patricia took a sip of her coffee. "We were at the ceremony yesterday. Do you think the man from England or Heather Clark would know anything about it?"

"I'm not sure," Debbie said. "I'm going to try to talk with anyone who might have an interest in it. Do you know Heather Clark?"

"I've worked with her professionally every so often. Of course, I had no idea her father served with Ray. It's funny that they were only a couple of hours away from each other all this time and didn't reconnect."

"Isn't it a shame? Ray would have liked that."

"Right before Carl left here, he mentioned he had no idea what happened to his father's World War II uniform," Patricia said. "And that he felt privileged yesterday to clean Ray's jacket because he'd never even seen his father's, except in a photo."

"Interesting." Debbie slid her purse off her shoulder. "He didn't say anything about that this morning."

"Maybe he didn't think it was relevant, since it was more of a musing than a fact related to the situation," Patricia said, putting on her attorney hat and using legal lingo as she pushed her empty plate to the middle of the table. "It seems several people might have had an interest in the jacket."

"Yes, that's true." Debbie and Patricia were thinking similarly. Debbie stepped forward and peered into Harry's half-full coffee cup. "I'll be right back to warm that up for you."

She stepped behind the counter, greeted Paulette at the espresso machine, and then ducked into the kitchen and said hello to Janet, who was cooking an omelet on the grill. She hung up her purse and grabbed an apron.

"How did it go?" Janet asked.

"Ray took it well, but I still want to fix this for him." Debbie tied her apron. "How have things been here?"

"Fine," Janet said. "We've been busy but not swamped."

Within a few minutes, that changed and every table in the café was full. The summer season had started. Debbie and Paulette hurried to take orders, fill drinks, and get the food out while Janet worked in the kitchen. Finally, by eleven, the last of the breakfast and brunch rush left.

"I wonder if the lunch rush will be that hectic." Janet poured herself a cup of coffee.

"Sit a minute and rest your feet," Debbie ordered her friend. Janet had already put in nearly a full shift considering the hours she spent baking before the café even opened.

"You sit down too, Debbie," Paulette said. "I'll finish wiping the tables."

Debbie poured herself a cup of coffee, grabbed her notebook and pen from her purse, and joined Janet at the far table.

Janet took a sip of coffee. "Any suspects for Ray's jacket, if it was indeed stolen?"

"No. But we can work on some ideas." Debbie flipped her notebook open. "Any chance Oliver Godfrey came in before I arrived?"

"I haven't seen him. Is he a suspect?"

"Not necessarily. I just want to make a list of people who might have an 'interest' in Ray's jacket, like Patricia said to me earlier. Oliver came all the way from England. Maybe he wanted a souvenir to take back."

"Wasn't he meeting with Ray this morning at ten?"

"That's right," Debbie said. "I wonder if he's still there."

"And Heather and Ruby went home to Columbus last night, right?"

"Yes, I assume they did. They left before dessert, around six fifteen or so, I think?"

Janet nodded.

Debbie started scribbling notes. "I'll still put Heather on the list. Maybe they stuck around somewhere in town. I think she would have ripped Ray's Purple Heart off his jacket yesterday if she could have gotten away with it."

As Debbie wrote, Janet said, "Carl stopped by and was lamenting not having his father's World War II jacket."

"That's what Patricia and Harry said." Debbie twirled the pen in her hand.

"Carl certainly had access to the jacket." Janet took another sip of coffee. "It disappeared from his shop."

"That's true." There wasn't video of anyone taking the jacket out either of the doors or the drive-up window, but Carl could have sneaked it out more easily than anyone.

Debbie wrote *Oliver Godfrey*, followed by *Heather Clark*. Then she added *Carl Miller* to the list. "You know who else has an interest in World War II uniforms?"

"Who?" Janet asked as she looked over the rim of her mug.

"Jonathon Bell."

"The news guy?"

Debbie nodded. "He collects World War II memorabilia by buying it online. He was shopping yesterday, maybe even during the ceremony. He made a bid on something online during the ceremony."

"That's not very attentive, for a news reporter."

"I was surprised too. It's probably part of the reason he was interested in Ray's story when I pitched it to him." Debbie added

Jonathon Bell to the list and then glanced back up at Janet. "That's four possible suspects."

"So far," Janet said.

Debbie set the pen down. "Heather's niece, Ruby, was with her."

"Do you think Ruby would have wanted the jacket?" Janet asked.

"I'm not sure, but Heather seemed to want Ruby to have the Purple Heart." Debbie picked up her mug. "Ruby is awfully shy. It's hard to imagine her doing something so daring."

Janet raised an eyebrow. "Ian often says the quiet ones are the ones to watch."

Debbie still couldn't imagine Ruby being involved. "I'll see if Oliver is with Ray at Good Shepherd, check in with Carl, and call Jonathon. Surely one of them will have some kind of information."

"Let's hope so," Janet said. "Ray's had that jacket for eighty years. It would be awful if it was gone for good."

Debbie remained at the table after Janet headed back to the kitchen. Besides Carl, none of the suspects resided locally. Oliver lived the farthest away. She needed to connect with him before he left town.

She took out her phone and called Ray. When he didn't answer, she called the front desk.

Someone picked up right away. "Good Shepherd Retirement Center. This is Ashley. How can I help you?"

"Ashley, it's Debbie Albright. I'm trying to get ahold of Ray. Have you seen him since breakfast?"

"He's here in the lobby."

"Oh, good. Is someone with him?" Maybe Oliver was there now.

"No," Ashley replied. "He is waiting for someone though."

Debbie's heart sank. "May I speak with him?"

"Sure. Hold on."

Ray came on the line. "Hello, Debbie. Any word on the jacket?"

"No, I'm afraid not." She sighed. "I called to see if Oliver Godfrey had stopped by, but from what Ashley said, I'm guessing he hasn't."

"That's right," Ray said. "I thought he would be here by now. It's almost lunchtime—he's nearly two hours late. I hope he's all right, but I don't think he's coming."

"I'll call the Oak Street Bed and Breakfast in Uhrichsville. He mentioned he was staying there," Debbie said. "I'll call you right back."

"You can leave a message for me at the front desk," Ray said. "Ashley will get it to me in the dining hall."

"I'll do that," Debbie said.

When Ray hung up, Debbie immediately looked up the phone number for the B and B, which their website said was run by a woman named Cindy Johnson. After a few rings, someone answered. "Hello?"

It was a child's voice, and Debbie was surprised, sure she had the wrong number. "Is this the Oak Street B and B?"

"Yeah."

Okay, then. "I'm calling to check on one of your guests, Oliver Godfrey."

"I'm not allowed to talk about the guests."

"I can understand that. Is Cindy Johnson around?"

"No."

"What's your name?"

"Loren."

"Is Cindy your grandmother?"

"Yes."

"I need to leave a message for her. Would you ask her to—"

The call disconnected.

Debbie stared at her phone. It would take just a few minutes to drive to the B and B. Surely someone besides Loren was in charge.

She ducked into the kitchen and grabbed her purse. "Janet, I need to run over to Uhrichsville. I'll be back as soon as I can."

"I'll be counting the seconds," Janet called as Debbie headed for the door.

When she reached the B and B, Debbie climbed out of her car, strode up the front steps, and knocked on the door. No one answered. She heard a noise and retreated down the front steps just as a woman came around the side of the house with a trowel in her hand.

"Hello!" The woman waved. "Can I help you?"

"I sure hope so. My name is Debbie Albright. I called about ten minutes ago. Are you Cindy Johnson?"

The woman nodded. "Yes. Did Loren answer the phone?"

"Yes," Debbie said.

Cindy shook her head. "Loren is my youngest grandson. He's eleven and doesn't always follow directions. I told him to let all calls go to voice mail. I needed to plant my daphne—it outgrew its pot." She brushed her hand against her jeans. "What do you need?"

"I'm searching for Oliver Godfrey. I know you can't give me any confidential information on him, but I was wondering if you could tell me whether he's still here."

Cindy appraised her, as if considering the request. Finally, she said, "He left. I found his key and a note on the front desk this morning."

"You didn't expect him to leave so soon?"

"No. He'd booked tonight too."

That didn't sound good for Oliver. "Did he say where he was going?"

"No." Cindy glanced around and lowered her voice. "Honestly, I found it all a little odd. He was so chatty yesterday when he checked in, so excited to visit Dennison. I was surprised to see his note and the key this morning. Why do you ask?"

"I had a question for him," Debbie answered. "If you hear from him, would you ask him to give me a call?" Debbie handed Cindy a business card with her number, wishing she'd given one to Oliver the day before. Or, better yet, that she'd gotten his number.

Janet had an appointment at two, so she left a little early. While Paulette waited on the lone couple left in the café, Debbie sat at a table and did a quick search for Oliver Godfrey and the island of Guernsey. An Oliver Godfrey popped up who had died in 1952. Definitely not the same Oliver Godfrey, though perhaps they were related. She couldn't find anything on a contemporary Oliver Godfrey, but then Oliver had mentioned that he hadn't lived on Guernsey for quite some time.

After more research, Debbie landed on the Isle of Guernsey Society website. She clicked the contact button and sent a message asking about an Oliver Godfrey who was the son of Adele Martin. She explained that he had been in Dennison, Ohio, for a ceremony honoring Ray Zink, an American World War II veteran who had served on Guernsey. Debbie asked for verification that Oliver was Adele's son and whether anyone had contact information for him.

She still wanted to talk to Carl and Jonathon, but for the moment, she returned to work. After all, she did have a business to run.

Right before closing, as Paulette got ready to leave, Eileen stepped through the door, followed by Ray and then Kim, who was pushing his wheelchair.

Debbie hurried to greet them. "Good afternoon. What can I get you?"

Eileen said, "I know you're about to close, but we wondered if we could sit and have a cup of coffee."

"Of course." Debbie motioned to the closest table.

Paulette stopped at the door. "I can stay."

"No, you go ahead. I can take care of this." Debbie stepped to the counter. "How about some Scottish shortbread to go with your coffee?"

"That sounds delicious," Eileen said as Kim pushed Ray up to the table closest to the counter. Then she and Eileen both sat down

Debbie studied her friends. Was Ray okay? He hadn't said a word. Eileen was doing all the talking. Debbie plated the shortbread, including one for herself, and then poured four cups of coffee.

As Debbie reached the table with her tray, Kim said, "Mom asked me to pick Ray and her up at Good Shepherd and bring them here, but she wouldn't say why." She touched her mother's arm. "What's going on?"

Eileen answered, "Ray has some things he wants to talk to you about. And we wanted Debbie to be part of the conversation."

Kim leaned toward Ray. "What is it? Is everything all right?"

Instead of answering, Ray turned to Debbie. "Did you tell her?"

"About the jacket?" Debbie shook her head. "I haven't had a chance yet."

"Tell me what?" Kim demanded.

"Would you tell her?" Ray asked Debbie. "It's still too fresh for me."

Debbie filled Kim in on the missing jacket, and then she said, "We don't have any leads yet. But I'm hoping we'll be able to figure out who took it and retrieve it soon." She explained that Ian had interviewed Carl and investigated the dry cleaners that morning. "I'm sure the only reason he let me be there with him and Carl is because I was a witness to Carl taking possession of the jacket," she concluded.

"Oh my," Kim murmured. "Ray, I'm so sorry."

"Thank you," Ray said. "Honestly, it's caused me to think about the future of that jacket and the other things I have from the war. A few photos. The letters my family and I exchanged. I have no one to leave those things to. Would you be interested in what I have for the museum's collection?"

"I'd definitely be interested in the photos and letters. And your jacket for a temporary exhibit. I already have quite a few uniforms in the permanent collection. More than I can display, honestly."

"Thank you. That's helpful information to have." Ray took a bite of shortbread before he spoke again. "I've been thinking so much about Normandy. And about my time in the Netherlands too. And the day the mine exploded on Guernsey. Leland Clark and I were together for all those events. I woke up thinking about him this morning. It's amazing how things that happened so long ago can still be so fresh in one's memory." A wry smile flashed across his face. "Especially when I can't remember what I had for breakfast."

They all laughed.

Kim reached across the table and patted his hand. "I imagine those events are deeply ingrained in in your subconscious."

"I guess so." Ray sighed. "I joined the 30th Infantry Division in the summer of 1943 in Camp Forest, Tennessee. It was a National Guard formation of soldiers from several states. We arrived in England in February 1944 and began training for the Allied invasion, although we didn't know where or when it would be. We landed on Omaha Beach after the first wave. I'd never imagined such horrors." He wrapped both hands around his mug.

Debbie shuddered, unable to picture them herself.

"You've read the books. Seen the movies. The point is, by some miracle, I survived. And so did Leland Clark. While so many others…" His voice faltered. "Anyway, I've thought of that today. But even more so the people we met along the way, the ones I'll never forget—no matter what."

CHAPTER FIVE

Normandy, France
June 22, 1944

On his nineteenth birthday, Ray hunkered down in his foxhole and reread letters from his sweetheart, Eleanor, that he'd managed to keep with him through his training in England, landing on Omaha Beach, and fighting their way through Normandy. He hadn't heard from Eleanor since January. His sister's letters had caught up with him. Why hadn't Eleanor's?

His platoon was in a hurry-up-and-wait mode. German snipers fired at them during the day, and enemy planes flew over at night. Compared to Omaha Beach, where they were sitting ducks, Ray felt relatively safe. Regardless, he was more on edge now, more alone—and scared—than at any other time in his entire life.

In Eleanor's last letter, she wrote of her work at the depot, how kind her boss, Eileen Turner, was, and how Eleanor missed singing to Ray's piano playing. No one plays like you do, *she'd written.* I dream of singing to your music. *He read the lines over and over.*

He switched to the letter dated May fourteenth that had just arrived from his sister, Gayle, who was twelve. She wrote about the Victory Garden she'd planted and how well it was growing, along with what was happening in the neighborhood. Everything we do is serenaded by locomotive whistles, *she wrote.* The constant coming and going of the trains is like a clock ticking all through town. We can't wait until one of those trains brings you home. *When had she learned to write so eloquently?*

Gayle had ended her letter with Happy birthday, big brother! Hopefully, this letter will reach you before you turn nineteen, but in case it gets delayed, I'll write that in every letter for the next month.

Smart girl.

There hadn't been a letter from his parents, but he guessed he'd get one soon. He'd been amazed that Gayle's letter had found him so quickly. It seemed to be a good sign that the mail had followed them across the channel from England. Hopefully he'd have a letter from Eleanor at next mail call.

"Zink!"

Ray glanced up, shading his eyes against the afternoon sun.

Sergeant Clark peered down at him. "Come with me." The sergeant was a few inches taller than Ray, quite a bit broader, and a few years older. He'd been a junior at the University of Kentucky when he'd been drafted, regardless of being enrolled in college. The army had become desperate for recruits.

When they were in England, training for the invasion, Sergeant Clark had said he'd complete his final year of college as soon as the war was over and then go to Harvard Law School.

Ray hadn't known anyone who'd gone to law school before. Clark's ambition impressed him. All Ray wanted to do was return to Dennison, marry Eleanor, and work to support his family. Once he got back home, he'd never leave again.

"Get moving!" Clark commanded.

Ray didn't want to. Whatever Clark had planned for him was sure to be risky. Ray would much rather stay in the foxhole. But Clark was his commanding officer, and it was Ray's duty to obey.

After tucking the letters back into his rucksack, Ray slung his rifle over his shoulder and hurried up the side of the foxhole, one hand on his helmet. "Where are we going?"

"In search of fresh food."

Ray's heart sank. Others had gone rummaging for food, which was understandable. The boxed rations were never enough. And never fresh. But Ray knew the French civilians, both farmers and those living in the nearby villages, had already endured years of the Germans stealing from them. He didn't want to take food from those who needed it. "Do you have money to buy the food, Sarge?"

"Of course. We're not thieves." Clark started off at a brisk march. "I've been watching you, Zink. Are you doing okay?"

"Yes," Ray answered.

"It's all right if you're not." Sergeant Clark increased his pace. "But the main thing is that you get your mind off of what's bothering you. That's why I asked you to accompany me."

Ray took a few quick steps, caught up with Clark, and then matched him stride for stride. He wouldn't let Sergeant Clark down. The man had been the platoon's fearless leader since he'd been put in charge, along with a first lieutenant, when the 30th Division arrived in Camp Atterbury to prepare to be shipped overseas.

Clark was a born leader with his imposing stature and booming voice. Even in the battle on Omaha Beach, he remained optimistic and resourceful. Ray and all the other men looked up to him.

The afternoon had grown warm, and Ray began to sweat. He couldn't help but note, even in the fresh air, that both he and Sergeant Clark needed to bathe. Another luxury—along with cots, roofs, and warm food—that they had left behind in England.

"There are a few houses past the woods," Sergeant Clark said. "Not quite a village. We'll see what we can find there."

As they came around a hedge, Ray spotted the houses, about ten in all, along with a few barns. He didn't see any livestock. Not even a chicken or two pecking around. A man walked behind a plow pulled by a scrawny horse in a field. It seemed late to plant a crop, but perhaps he hadn't been able to earlier in the spring. Every day, Ray thanked God the war hadn't reached the United States, that his parents and sister and Eleanor were all safe. At least from invasion and battles right outside their doors. The losses of the French people tugged at his heart.

Sergeant Clark moved his rifle into position as they neared the house and called out, "Bonjour!"

When no one responded, he led the way to the front door and opened it. "Bonjour," he called again. "We're American soldiers."

Again there was no response. Ray followed Clark into the house, his heart racing. A table and two chairs stood in what appeared to be a living area, but no one was there. It could be a trap. Maybe Germans lurked in the next room, ready to capture them—or worse.

But the next room was empty. The third room had a chimney in the ceiling but no stove, and a counter area but no sink. It appeared whoever had lived there had moved out.

"Why don't we go ask the farmer if he has anything to sell?" Ray suggested.

They exited the house and starting walking toward the field. When they reached it, Ray saw that the man had turned at the end of a row and was midway across the field with his back to them.

Clark stopped at the split-rail fence and called out to him, but the farmer either didn't hear him or pretended not to.

"May I help you?"

Ray whirled around, his hand on his rifle even as he registered the voice was female and spoke English with an accent.

Sergeant Clark turned too but responded with a cheery, "Bonjour, mademoiselle."

The young woman standing by the beech tree appeared to be about Ray's age. She wore a summer dress and men's boots that were too large. She carried a basket in one hand and a jug in the other.

"Bonjour," she replied to Sergeant Clark and then, again in English, she asked, "What do you need?"

"Fresh food," Clark answered. "Eggs, meat, produce. Anything we can buy from you." He nodded toward the farmer. "Is that your father?"

"No," she answered. "He's my..." She hesitated, as if searching for the correct term. "Grand uncle." She motioned to a house to the north. "Perhaps my mother can help you. Follow me."

Ray tagged along behind the young woman.

Sergeant Clark, on the other hand, walked beside her, asking all sorts of questions. "How old are you?"

"Twenty," she answered.

"When did you learn English?"

"As a child at my school in Paris."

"Paris?" Sergeant Clark sounded surprised.

"Yes, we came here before the Germans invaded in the spring of 1940—my mother spent summers here as a girl."

"Who are you living with?"

"My mother and sister. And uncle."

"How were you treated by the Germans?"

Instead of answering the last question, she turned toward a stucco three-story house.

Clark said, "I'm Sergeant Leland Clark. What is your name?"

"Alié," she answered.

"Do you have a surname?"

"Dumas."

Clark didn't introduce Ray—and Ray didn't introduce himself.

Alié led the way around the house to the back. An older woman, with her gray hair twisted into a bun at the nape of her neck, stood at a clothesline with a laundry basket at her feet, hanging a threadbare towel.

"Maman," Alié said and then began speaking in French as the woman faced them, first with an expression of fear on her face and then resignation.

The woman responded in French, tucking a stray strand of hair behind her ear.

Alié turned to Sergeant Clark. "We hid some food from the Germans in the house. But you must pay. We need money to get back to Paris."

Sergeant Clark reached into his pocket and took out a wad of American bills. "We will pay."

The older woman left the basket and led the way to the house and into the kitchen. A girl around Gayle's age sat at the table, wrapped in a woven blanket.

"This is my mother, Madame Dumas, and my sister, Anne."

Sergeant Clark and Ray greeted both the mother and sister. Alié turned to Sergeant Clark again. "I know you're interested in ages. Anne is twelve—and ill."

"What's wrong with her?" Ray asked.

Alié smirked. "The quiet one speaks." She put a hand on Anne's shoulder. "We can't afford a doctor, nor are there many around, but we know it's her heart. She had scarlet fever three years ago."

Ray felt a stab in his own heart. Every family feared scarlet fever and the lasting effects some struggled with.

Anne didn't smile, but she nodded to Ray.

Alié led the way into a living room. It was empty except for a piano along the interior wall. Ray veered to it and ran his fingers along the ivory keys.

"Do you play?" Alié asked.

"Yes," Ray answered.

"Would you play now?"

"Yes." He turned to the older woman and gestured to the piano. "With your permission."

"Oui," she answered.

Ray pulled out the bench, sat, and placed his hands on the keys. He closed his eyes and for a moment felt as if he were home, waiting to hear Eleanor's ethereal voice.

"Go ahead," Alié said.

He began to play "As Time Goes By." When the verse started, Alié began to sing along. Her voice wasn't as clear or strong as Eleanor's, but it was beautiful. Moved, Ray leaned into his playing, matching the emotion in the young woman's voice. For the first time in months, his loneliness and fears began to fade away until he was entirely living in the present in a house in Normandy, France, without a thought in the world except the music coming from his fingers on the piano keys.

When he played the last note, Madame Dumas began to clap. "Bravo!" she called, then added something in French.

Alié translated. "Maman says, 'It's been so long since we've had music in our house.'"

Ray's face grew warm. "Merci, Madame Dumas."

As Ray scooted the bench back underneath the piano, Anne said, "Don't stop."

But then a shot rang out, and Anne flung herself to the floor.

Alié rushed to the window. "Grand-Oncle!" She turned and tore through the front door.

Sergeant Clark rushed after her.

CHAPTER SIX

Ray knocked the piano bench over in his hurry to follow Alié. Manners told him to pick it up, but this was an emergency. He ran instead, holding his rifle in position. His heart raced as he barreled out the door.

Clark had taken a position at the side of the house and aimed his rifle at a knoll to the north while Alié ran toward the field. Her great-uncle continued with his work as if nothing had happened. Obviously, neither he nor the horse had been hit, for which Ray was grateful.

"Cover me!" Clark barked.

"Yes, sir!" Ray moved into position as Clark, staying low, moved closer to the top of the hill. Ray held the rifle in his right hand and took his binoculars out of his pants pocket with his left. He pointed them toward the knoll. He squinted and made out a barricade of wood. One lone German soldier stood behind it and raised his own pair of binoculars.

Ray aimed his rifle at the man, but the soldier crouched before he could line up a shot. A few seconds later the man rushed to the top of the knoll and then disappeared down the other side. Ray whistled at Sergeant Clark and motioned for him to return. Clark did, and Ray explained what he'd seen.

"We should go back and report what's going on," Clark said. "There could be a German nest on the other side."

Alié was returning from the field, leading the horse. Her great-uncle maneuvered the plow, but it seemed he was reluctant to stop for the day.

The uncle acknowledged Sergeant Clark and Ray with a nod. He was stooped and had nearly snow-white hair that needed cutting. His brown eyes were cloudy and his skin leathered.

Alié helped him unhitch the horse, and then the uncle led it toward the barn, leaving the plow behind.

"His hearing is bad," she said, as if explaining why he hadn't seemed frightened.

"Do the Germans often come down from that hill?" Sergeant Clark asked Alié.

"Not for the last few days," she answered. "We thought they'd left but apparently not."

Sergeant Clark dug the money out of his pocket again. "Could we come back this evening to collect the food?"

WHISTLE STOP CAFÉ MYSTERIES

"Yes," Alié answered. "We have eggs, a couple of chickens we can spare, last year's potatoes and turnips, and early peas. Even a few strawberries."

Ray's mouth watered.

Sergeant Clark scanned their surroundings. "Where do you keep your chickens? And the food?"

"The chickens roost in an upstairs room during the day," Alié explained. "We let them out at night. Our garden is spread out in quite a few small patches. We keep the potatoes and turnips upstairs too. We told the Germans Anne had tuberculous, and they haven't come in the house since then." She glanced from Clark to Ray. "I can't tell you how relieved we are to have you Americans arrive. Finally, we have hope."

Pride swelled in Ray, and Clark smiled and handed several bills to Alié. "We'll be back in a few hours."

"We'll have the food ready for you," she answered.

"Stay inside," Clark said.

"We will."

When they reached camp, Clark went straight to Lieutenant Cohen, who then communicated the information to his commanding officer. Ray expected their platoon might be sent to clear out the Germans, but after a couple of hours they hadn't received any such orders.

After eating rations for supper—a biscuit with canned meat and a chocolate bar—Sergeant Clark said to Ray, "Let's go get the food before it gets dark."

The two emptied their rucksacks into their foxholes and slipped away, following the same route they had taken earlier in the day. When they reached the group of houses, they went straight to Alié's back door.

Clark knocked quietly, and the door was opened immediately.

"Come in," Alié said. "Quickly."

Ray's mouth watered at the scent of roasted chicken.

Once they were inside, Sergeant Clark asked, "Why the secrecy?"

"Two German soldiers came down the hill and were poking around in the barn," Alié said. "Hopefully they've returned to their post and haven't seen you."

Bundles of food covered the kitchen table. Sergeant Clark took off his rucksack and opened it. Ray did the same.

Alié's mother took Sergeant Clark's rucksack and Alié took Ray's, and they began filling them with roasted potatoes and turnips. Alié pulled away the paper wrapper of one of the bundles, revealing a roasted chicken surrounded by eggs.

"The eggs are boiled," she explained. "That way they won't make a mess if they break."

She wound some twine around the bundle to once again secure it and then placed it at the top of Ray's pack while her mother placed a small woven basket of strawberries and peas on the top of Clark's.

"Merci," Clark said, pulling out more money.

Alié's mother retrieved one last package from the table. "Fromage," she explained, and tucked the cheese into the pocket of Clark's pack. Then she turned to Ray and pointed toward the living room. "Musique?"

"Isn't it too loud?"

"No," Alié said. "Anne used to play before she fell ill. No one came to check who was playing."

"Is that all right?" Ray asked Sergeant Clark.

"I think one song would be fine." He smiled at Alié. "As long as you sing along."

Alié led the way into the living room, where Anne, still wrapped in the blanket, sat on the window ledge. The great-uncle was sitting in a straight-backed chair with a book in his hand.

Ray sat at the piano. "What would you like me to play, Alié?"

"Do you know 'Down Forget-Me-Not Lane'?"

"I do," he answered.

He began to play, and Alié began to sing about rainy days and rainbows and singing to keep the troubles away.

It felt as if that rainbow was still a long way off, but as the song went on, Ray felt more optimistic. That was what music did for him—and so many others too.

Ray stole a glance at Alié. She sang with her eyes closed, as lost in the music as he was. Madame Dumas stood behind her, and Anne was smiling. Their great-uncle wasn't smiling, but he no longer appeared as dour either. Sergeant Clark gazed at Alié as if he was afraid she might disappear if he looked away.

As Alié sang the last line, Ray took in the room again. He would never forget this moment—playing the piano in a French farmhouse in Normandy, days after the Allied forces' invasion. He didn't know what was ahead, but he'd treasure this memory of simple beauty after the storm. Always.

Once he finished, he let his fingertips rest on the ivory keys. When would he play again?

"Regrettably, we need to go," Sergeant Clark said, still gazing at Alié.

She opened her eyes and nodded. Then she put her hand on Ray's shoulder and said, "Merci. I forgot how wonderful music makes me feel."

Ray understood what she meant. He stood and reached for her hand to shake it. But she offered it to him with her palm down. He raised her hand to his lips and kissed it with gratitude.

It made him miss Eleanor even more.

Once they'd entered the woods on the other side of the house, Clark said, "Isn't Alié something? She's as beautiful as she is brave."

Ray nodded in agreement and then asked, "Do you have a sweetheart back home?"

"One or two." Clark laughed. "None as striking as Alié. How about you?"

Ray hadn't mentioned Eleanor to the others. She seemed too precious to talk about, and he didn't want the others teasing him—or demeaning her, as some did about other sweethearts. He wasn't sure whether he should change that now.

"Do you?" Sergeant Clark pressed.

Ray couldn't think of any answer to give but the truth. "Yes. Her name is Eleanor."

"Does she sing?"

"Yes," Ray answered.

"As beautifully as Alié?"

"Yes," Ray said, though privately he preferred Eleanor's voice. "Both Eleanor and Alié have beautiful voices."

"Lucky you," Sergeant Clark said.

His next words were cut off when gunfire erupted behind them.

Both men ducked behind trees. "It's not close, but we need to go back," Clark hissed. "What if the Germans are attacking Alié's house?"

Ray agreed. "We should leave our packs here." He shrugged out of his and placed it behind a tree.

"Good idea." Clark did the same. Then the two darted from tree to tree to the edge of the woods, holding their rifles in position. Dusk had fallen enough to show gunfire on the knoll as they reached the farmland around the houses.

It appeared an attack was taking place. Had the rest of the platoon been sent to clear out the German nest?

Sergeant Clark dashed to the back door with Ray right behind him and knocked softly.

A few seconds later, Alié opened the door.

"Are you all right?" Clark asked.

"Yes," she whispered. "Your soldiers are winning. We've been watching from the upstairs window." As she spoke to Clark, she waved to Ray. Then she smiled. "Bonne nuit."

"Good night," Ray replied softly.

"We'll check on you tomorrow," Clark said.

Alié waved again, and they turned to leave. As Ray followed Clark back into the woods, the sergeant said over his shoulder, "Isn't this an amazing adventure?"

Ray suppressed a smile. That wasn't the way he'd describe it, but he could understand how Sergeant Clark viewed the happenings of the day that way. Ray simply wanted to do his duty and stay alive.

When they reached their platoon with the food, everyone was accounted for. It turned out another platoon had been sent to attack the German nest. As they climbed down the side of the foxhole, one of the privates said, "I smell chicken."

Sergeant Clark put his backpack on the ground. "You're all in for a treat."

Ray slid off his rucksack. "Should I open it up?"

"Go ahead, Zink."

Ray had never felt like such a hero. He took out the package of chicken and eggs. "Bradford, open your knife and pass it over here." He cut the twine binding the package, his mouth watering as he did.

Bradford and the others groaned.

"We've brought you a feast." Clark pulled some potatoes and turnips from his pack. As he brought out the cheese, Lieutenant Cohen appeared in the dark.

"What's going on here?" he asked.

Clark grinned up at him. "I brought you something." He tossed the cheese to him. "Enjoy."

Lieutenant Cohen sniffed the package and smiled. "Merci, Clark."

Clark saluted him and then tossed him a potato too.

Ray was sorry to see the cheese go but thankful their lieutenant didn't demand more of the food.

They all fell asleep with full bellies that night, and even though they awoke to a drizzle, the men were happy. As Ray said his morning prayers, he thanked the Lord for Sergeant Clark. He was the kind of leader who was easy to follow.

Ray hadn't told anyone it was his nineteenth birthday. Thanks to Leland Clark, it had been a good one after all.

CHAPTER SEVEN

*A*fter Ray, Eileen, and Kim left, Debbie finished cleaning the café and preparing for the next day. Paulette had said goodbye right after the trio had arrived.

As she finished, Janet stopped by. "Good, you're still here. I was out running errands and kept thinking about Ray's jacket. Is there anything I can do to help?"

"I was going to head over to the dry cleaners. I'm hoping to talk to Elwood. Want to come with me?"

"Sure." Janet dangled her keys. "I'll drive."

When they arrived, Carl stood at the counter.

Behind him, his brother, Elwood, operated the first machine.

"Hello, ladies," Carl said in greeting. "Do you have any news?"

Debbie shook her head. "We stopped by to see if you'd remembered anything more."

Carl shook his head. "I feel positively ill about it."

Elwood, who had a fringe of gray hair around his bald head, stepped away from the machine toward the counter. "Hello, Debbie, Janet." He pointed to the rack. "When we left yesterday, Ray's jacket was hanging right there. We took off the medals to clean the jacket, but it was dry enough to reattach them before we left. I wish we had called you to pick it up last night."

So did she. But there was no way to know then that the jacket would vanish. "What time did you leave yesterday?"

Elwood glanced at Carl. "Was it around seven?"

"Seven thirty, I think." That was what he had said earlier in the day too.

"Carl said your father served in World War II," Janet said to Elwood.

"He did," Elwood said.

Janet pushed back a lock of her blond hair. "It's a shame you don't have his uniform."

"We do have it," Elwood said. "It's in his trunk up in my attic. I saw it up there at least twenty years ago."

Carl crossed his arms. "I didn't know you had it. My mom said it was lost at some point."

"No." Elwood smiled at Janet. "Carl's eighteen years younger than I am. Our father married his mother after my mother passed away."

Debbie asked, "When did your father pass away?"

Carl answered, "When I was five."

Elwood nodded. "In 1974 to be exact. I'd been working with him here and took over." Debbie had never thought about how old Elwood was, but that account put him in his early seventies. He and his wife had operated the dry cleaners for as long as she could remember. Now they were turning it over to Carl.

Carl asked, "How did Ray handle the news?"

"With as much optimism as he handles everything else," Debbie answered. "He expects the jacket will turn up."

"Am I a suspect?" Carl dropped his arms to his side. "Is that why you stopped by again?"

"I wouldn't say you're a suspect," Debbie said. "But you were the last person to see the jacket. Anything you can remember could be helpful."

"He was one of the last people to see the jacket," Elwood corrected her. "I was the other. I'm as much of a suspect as he is. We left at the same time last night. Sylvie had dinner ready when we arrived. She'll confirm what time we got home. In fact, she can show you proof of that, and that we didn't have any jacket with us."

"Would you be willing to talk to Ian?" Janet asked Elwood.

"I'd be happy to answer any of Ian's questions that I can. He's welcome to search this property and our house. Whatever it takes. We want that jacket found as much as anyone else, for Ray's sake. But also for our own. It doesn't look good to have a garment stolen from our shop, especially an irreplaceable one like a World War II veteran's jacket."

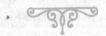

On their way out of the dry cleaners, Janet asked, "So what do you think? Are Carl and Elwood suspects?"

"Elwood certainly didn't sound like one, offering to have the shop and their house searched. And telling us to go talk to Sylvie."

"I need to get home and start dinner," Janet said. "But I'll drop you off at the Millers' if you want."

Over the roof of Janet's car, Debbie said, "Thanks. I think talking to Sylvie would be a good idea."

A few minutes later, Debbie headed up the driveway to Sylvie Miller's kitchen door. Debbie's mother was friends with Sylvie, and there had been a few times over the years when Debbie had stopped to drop something off for her.

When she reached the kitchen door, which was on the side of the house along the driveway, she found it wide open. A throw rug came flying out of it and landed behind the back bumper of the Millers' car.

"Hello," Debbie called through the door, hoping another throw rug wasn't about to follow the first.

Sylvie poked her head out the door. Her mop of gray curls was pulled up in a scarf. "Debbie, what are you doing here?" Her smile quickly faded. "Is this about Ray's missing jacket?"

"Elwood sent me to talk with you. This doesn't sound good, but—"

"He and Carl were the last two people to see the jacket," Sylvie finished for her. "I've expected Ian to stop by all day."

"I imagine he will," Debbie said. "Speaking of Elwood, he said you have proof that he and Carl didn't have the jacket with them last night."

"I didn't see them carry anything into the house, but I don't know what proof he's talking about."

"Any chance you have video of it?" Debbie suggested.

"Oh, that." She took her phone from her apron pocket. "Elwood put cameras on both doors here at the house when he installed them at the shop. Let me see. Here's the app." She held up the phone and showed a video of Elwood and Carl coming in the back door at 7:38 p.m. Elwood carried a small paper bag, and Carl carried a water bottle. Neither had anything resembling a jacket or something that could have concealed the jacket.

"Thank you," Debbie said.

Sylvie slid the phone back into her pocket. "Of course, if they had Ray's jacket, they wouldn't bring it into the house in full view, would they?"

Debbie gave a wry smile. "Probably not. Do you think they took the jacket?"

"Elwood wouldn't. Not in a million years. I'm not sure about Carl."

Debbie cocked her head. She'd expected Sylvie's response about Elwood, but the admission about her brother-in-law startled her.

Sylvie motioned toward the kitchen. "Can you come in for a cup of tea?"

"I'd like that." Debbie hoped she didn't sound too eager, but if Sylvie had information that implicated Carl in the disappearance of the jacket, she needed to know what it was.

Five minutes later, Debbie sat across from Sylvie at a small table under the kitchen window. A pot of blooming violets sat in the middle of the table, along with the pot of steeping tea.

"I need to tell you about Carl," Sylvie said. "Elwood's father remarried rather quickly after his first wife passed away. Carl was born a year later when Elwood was a senior in high school. He and I had just started dating. Elwood's father owned the dry cleaners and hoped Elwood would go to work with him and then take over the business someday, but that day came sooner than we could have imagined."

Debbie had heard something similar from the brothers.

"He passed away five years later, after we'd been married a couple of years. We took over the dry cleaners, and Elwood's stepmom took Carl and moved to Pittsburgh. We had our girls, raised them, and had very little contact with Carl or his mother—until about ten years ago. She had passed away, and Carl wanted a relationship with Elwood."

The two men hadn't gone into these details. Debbie all but perched on the edge of her seat, anxious to soak up every word.

"Then Carl fell on hard times a year ago. The international corporation he was working for downsized. He's in his midfifties, so it's been hard for him to find another job. Our girls don't want the dry-cleaning business, and I can't imagine either of them moving back to Dennison. They've built homes and lives elsewhere."

"That makes sense," Debbie replied. Not so long ago, she'd felt the same way.

"Elwood and I are over seventy now." Sylvie smiled as she cleared her throat. "Seventy-three, actually. Who knows how long we can keep going? So we offered Carl a deal. Elwood will keep helping as long as he can, and Carl will make payments to us to buy the business over the next decade."

"That sounds like a good plan."

Sylvie rose and poured out the tea then handed a cup to Debbie. "And for now, Carl is living with us."

"How is that going?" Debbie took a sip of tea.

"Well enough. Although I hope he finds another place eventually." She leaned forward. "What I really hope is that he finds a wife."

Debbie smiled but felt apprehensive. Surely Sylvie didn't think she was a candidate. Debbie put her cup on the table. "You mentioned that you weren't sure whether Carl might have taken the jacket. Do you think he did? He thought his father's jacket had been lost, but Elwood said today that it's in your attic."

"I didn't know Carl thought it had been lost, but yes, it's in our attic. It's sad when you think of all the things Carl missed out on by not growing up here. Memories he could have had with Elwood. He missed his nieces knowing him as their uncle. He's unmoored in so many ways. He lived overseas for most of his adult life. He worked as an accountant for the same company in Zurich, Johannesburg, and Amsterdam."

"Amsterdam? Do you think the fact that Ray served and was wounded in the Netherlands would have resonated with Carl?"

"I don't know," Sylvie said. "But I think coming to Dennison, a place he left when he was five, has been complicated for him."

"Complicated enough to steal a World War II veteran's jacket?"

Sylvie shrugged. "It's hard to say. I'm not saying I think he did it. I'm just saying I don't know him well enough to guess whether he would or not."

"If he did take it, what would he have done with it?"

"He wouldn't have brought it here."

"What kind of car does he drive?"

"He came here straight from Amsterdam and hasn't bought a car yet. He's borrowed ours a few times."

"Did he leave the house last night?"

Sylvie pulled out her phone again and rechecked her security camera footage. "There's no evidence of it. He's staying in the back bedroom. He would have had to turn off the system before he could go through a door, and I know he didn't do that because the keypad is in Elwood's and my bedroom. We have the windows on the security system also, so the app would let me know if his was opened last night."

Of course, Elwood could have turned off the security system and gotten out of the house, but she didn't think it was plausible that a seventy-something would climb a tree and crawl through the ventilation window at the dry cleaners. Sylvie's explanation seemed to exonerate Carl—at least from stealing the jacket during the night.

Even if Carl had somehow managed to bypass the home security system and then gotten into the dry cleaners, he would have then had to stash the jacket somewhere besides his brother's house. It didn't sound like he had access to a hiding spot.

It seemed unlikely one of them took the jacket, but that didn't mean it was impossible. Could she rule either one out altogether?

As Debbie walked home, she tried Ian, but her call went straight to voice mail. She told him about Oliver mysteriously leaving the B and B that morning and what she'd found out about Carl and Elwood. Sylvie believed Carl was unsettled, but there wasn't any evidence that he had taken the jacket.

Then she called the TV studio and asked to speak with Jonathon Bell, but he was unavailable. She left a message asking him to call her back as soon as possible.

As she passed the depot, her phone rang. She was delighted to see Greg's name on the screen.

She answered cheerfully. "Hello. How has your day been?"

"Great. Want to join us for dessert after Jaxon's game? Julian made brownies."

"I'd love to. What time?"

"How about eight? We'll eat outside."

"Sounds great. See you then." Besides the few dates they'd managed to go on in the last month, getting together with Greg usually meant going to his boys' basketball, football, and baseball games. Sitting together in church. A barbecue in his backyard every once in a while. She was thankful for whatever worked for him, whether or not it was an official date or time with him and the boys. His kids had to be the priority even though they were in their teens and could certainly be left on their own. They needed time with their dad.

When she arrived that evening, Greg's older son, Jaxon, was dressed in his basketball uniform, and his younger son, Julian, wore his usual shorts, T-shirt, and tennis shoes. They were shooting hoops in the driveway.

She called out hello, and Julian caught the ball and tucked it under his arm. "Hi, Debbie. Dad's in the backyard." He nudged Jaxon. "Let's go eat my brownies."

Julian darted to the gate and opened it for Debbie. They went around the house and found Greg lighting a citronella candle that sat on the picnic table. Hammer, the family's black-and-white border collie, gave a welcoming bark and raced to greet her.

Debbie reached down and scratched the dog's head. "Hey, buddy. Good to see you too."

The Connors' backyard was an oasis with an expansive lawn, a large patio with a sectional around a firepit, a barbecue area with a grill, and a table with a shade umbrella. The boys reached the table before she did.

"Hey." Greg met her with a hug. "Jaxon, would you get the ice cream out of the freezer?"

"Sure." Jaxon went into the house.

"We're going to watch a movie after dessert," Julian said. "Want to watch it with us?"

Debbie sat down at the table. "What are you watching?"

"*A Bridge Too Far.* It's about a battle Mr. Zink fought in."

Debbie glanced at Greg.

"Not exactly," he said. "Mr. Zink was wounded at Valkenburg along the Geul River after the Nazis blew up a bridge, right after the 30th Division entered the Netherlands. The movie is about what happened after that."

Debbie was impressed that Greg could rattle off so much information about Ray's time in the Netherlands.

"Oh," Julian said. "So it's about another bridge the Nazis blew up?"

Greg began cutting the brownies. "It's definitely about another bridge—one that was part of the Battle of Arnhem. You'll have to see what happened on the bridge."

Jaxon returned with the ice cream, and the boys sat down at the table. Greg served the brownies, and Julian heaped two scoops of ice cream on top of each one.

After Greg finished his dessert, he said, "Boys, I'm going to show you your great-grandfather's Purple Heart. I'll be right back."

Through a mouthful of brownie, Julian asked his brother, "Is that the thing in that weird box Dad keeps in his bottom drawer?"

Jaxon wrinkled his nose. "Why were you snooping in Dad's dresser?"

"I was looking for clean socks."

Debbie did her best not to smile but didn't quite succeed.

"Yeah, that's the thing." Jaxon raised his eyebrow. "His clean socks are in the top drawer."

Julian took the last bite of his brownie and then said, "I know that now."

Greg returned with a shadow box.

"Yep, that's it," Julian said.

"You've seen it before?" Greg answered.

Julian's face reddened. "Maybe."

Greg's eyebrows shot up, but he didn't press the matter.

Julian quickly changed the subject. "Did Great-Grandpa fight with Mr. Zink?"

Greg shook his head. "No. My grandfather fought with the US 1st Infantry Division. He died in Tunisia during the Battle of El Guettar in March 1943."

"Where is Tunisia?" Julian asked.

"In northern Africa," Greg said.

"Was he buried in Dennison?"

Greg shook his head. "No. I'm not sure where he was buried. I'm guessing somewhere close to where he died."

Julian piped up, "But he helped save the world from the Nazis, right?"

"That's right," Greg replied. "He absolutely did."

"That must have been really hard for Grandpa to lose his dad like that," Jaxon said.

"Your grandpa never knew his father. He was born after Great-Grandpa Earl left for the war, but it was still hard on him. It was a loss for him his entire life, even though he had a good stepdad."

The boys knew what it was like to lose a parent. Their mother had died six years before from cancer.

Greg opened the back of the shadow box and removed the Purple Heart. He carefully handed it to Julian then pulled a second medal from the box. "This is Great-Grandpa Earl's Bronze Star."

Julian asked, "What is that for?"

Greg handed the Bronze Star to Jaxon. "I'm not sure, exactly. He must have done something above and beyond the call of duty."

Debbie took out her phone and looked it up. "It says here 'the Bronze Star is given for heroism, outstanding achievement, or meritorious service.'"

"Which one of those do you think he got a Bronze Star for?" Jaxon asked.

"I have no idea," Greg answered.

Jaxon wrapped his hand around the Bronze Star. "Why don't you know?"

"No one ever told me."

Jaxon opened his hand and stared at the Bronze Star. "Can you find out?"

Greg glanced at Debbie. "Do you think that's possible?"

"Maybe," she answered. "Do you want me to look into it?"

"Would you?"

"Of course." Debbie enjoyed that sort of research.

"Does Mr. Zink have a Bronze Star too?" Julian asked.

"I'm not sure," Greg said.

Debbie nodded. "Yes, he does," she said. She had seen it on his jacket with his other medals.

"Thanks, Dad." Jaxon handed the Bronze Star to Greg. "These are really cool. I'm glad we have them to remember Great-Grandpa Earl."

"Yeah." Julian handed the Purple Heart back to Greg. "Can we start the movie now?"

"You bet." Greg returned the medals back to the box. "Debbie, have you decided if you want to stay for the movie?"

Without hesitating, she answered, "I'd love to."

CHAPTER EIGHT

T he next morning, Debbie arrived at the Whistle Stop ready for a busy Saturday breakfast rush, expecting both tourists and locals.

Janet greeted her in the kitchen. "Look what I found." She held up an apron covered with a strawberry print. "I ordered three of them. Yours and Paulette's are on your hooks."

"They're so cute," Debbie said. The aprons were perfect for the month of June. And Janet planned to make several specialty items featuring strawberries throughout the month.

As Debbie started the coffee with her new apron tied around her waist, she thought about Greg's grandfather, Earl Connor. She didn't know anything about the Battle of El Guettar.

But what a loss to his loved ones. And that had been multiplied countless times over. Earl Connor Sr. was only one of millions upon millions of soldiers who had died in World War II.

She'd start by going through the newspaper archives at the library and see what she could find about Earl Sr. Surely there was a big write-up when he passed away and another when he was awarded the Purple Heart and the Bronze Star. At one time the family probably had copies of the articles, but over the years maybe they had been misplaced or accidentally thrown away.

In the middle of the breakfast rush, Debbie's phone buzzed. She scooped it from her apron pocket. Jonathon Bell. She pressed the red icon and put her phone back into her pocket. She'd have to return his call when business slowed.

By ten thirty, the breakfast and brunch crowd had thinned enough for Debbie to take a break. She ducked out into the lobby and tried Jonathon, but he didn't answer. When she got his voice mail, she left him a message to call her back after three.

Shortly before three, as they were preparing to close, Ian came into the café. "I'm here, love," he called. That made the few customers left in the café smile, and one laughed.

Janet waved at him from behind the counter. "What would you like?"

"A cup of tea and a piece of your shortbread."

"I'll get the tea." Debbie poured the boiling water into a stainless-steel pot and then dunked the bag. After months of practice, she knew exactly how Ian liked his tea. She grabbed a mug and put both in front of Ian. Then she poured a small pitcher of milk as Janet brought out the shortbread.

"How is your day going?" Janet asked him.

"All right. Busy."

"Any word about the shoe print?" Debbie asked, though she knew he wouldn't share specifics of that information with her if he had learned anything.

Ian shook his head.

"Have you gotten in touch with Heather?"

He gave her another smile and poured himself some more tea.

Debbie poured herself a cup of coffee. "I had an interesting conversation with Sylvie Miller yesterday afternoon." She relayed what Sylvie had said about Carl.

"Do you think that's significant?"

"I have no idea, but I wanted to pass it on to you anyway," Debbie said. "I don't see how either of the brothers could climb the tree and get through the window, let alone get down from the cabinet and then back up. Elwood is anxious for you to solve who took the jacket, for Ray's sake but also for their business. He's expressed that you're welcome to do a more thorough search of the building and even their house."

"I don't think it's come to that yet." He finished his tea and then said, "Tell Janet I'll see her at home, okay?"

"Will do." Debbie picked up his cup and plate.

"Thanks." As Ian went through the café door, Janet came out of the kitchen. "I overheard a conversation Ian had with Graham, Heather Clark's assistant, last night. He was in the study and had the call on speaker."

"What did he say?"

"That Heather was sorry to hear the jacket had gone missing but she didn't have any information that would assist the investigation." Janet shoved her hands into the pockets of her apron. "Or something like that."

"So a canned response?"

Janet nodded. "Straight from the politician's mouth."

An hour later, Debbie stepped into the Claymont Public Library and headed straight to the newspaper collection index. She searched for *Earl Connor Sr.* and came across an obituary from March 23, 1943. That was all. She requested the microfiche from the librarian and threaded it through the machine.

The obituary was located on page three. Debbie read through it.

Earl Gregory Connor was born in New Philadelphia, Ohio, in 1917 and moved to Dennison with his family in 1923. He graduated from Dennison High School in 1935 and married Vivian Olson in 1936. They had four children. Earl Sr. was inducted into the US Army in May of 1942 and died during the Battle of El Guettar in Tunisia on March 23, 1943. He is survived by his parents, William and Mary Connor, his wife, Vivian, and their four children, all under six years old.

Vivian had been a widow with four small children to raise on her own. What a daunting task.

Debbie printed out the article so she could reference it as often as she needed to. There was no mention of a Purple Heart or Bronze Star, but the obituary had run mere weeks after Earl Sr.'s death. The medals probably hadn't been awarded by then.

As Debbie left the library and stepped into the afternoon sunshine, her phone rang with a call from Jonathon Bell.

She answered it. "Hello, Jonathon. Thank you for getting back to me."

"Well, with a mysterious message about a missing jacket, how could I not? Did you say Ray's World War II jacket is missing?"

"Yes." Debbie reached her car and leaned against it. "Did you hear anyone mention it on Thursday? Did anyone say anything to you?"

"No. Why would anyone take Ray's jacket?"

"We don't know," Debbie said. "It went missing from the dry cleaners."

"Sounds like an inside job," Jonathon said. "I hope that's being investigated."

Debbie didn't want to say too much. "Yes, our police are very thorough," she said.

"As far as hearing anything on Thursday, I didn't. I interviewed the guy from Guernsey though."

"Oliver Godfrey," Debbie supplied.

"Yes, that's his name," Jonathon said. "Have you spoken to him about the jacket? He made a comment about how much he admired it."

"Not yet," Debbie said.

"Why not?"

"He left Dennison the next morning, a day earlier than he said he was going to, before I had a chance to contact him."

"That sounds suspicious."

Debbie didn't respond. She wasn't about to give Jonathon the opportunity to take her words as an official statement.

"How about if I do a story about the missing jacket?" Jonathon suggested. "I could come over there on Monday morning and interview Ray. That would give the case publicity. There's a chance that whoever took it will get spooked and return it. Would eleven o'clock work?"

"I'll check with Ray," Debbie answered.

"Just text me and let me know one way or the other," Jonathon said. "I'm going to an auction tonight."

"All right," Debbie said. "I'll do that."

"Bye!" Jonathon ended the call.

Debbie climbed into her car and called Ray. He answered after a few rings.

"Hello?" His voice sounded groggy.

"It's Debbie. Did I wake you?"

"I'm not sure," Ray said. "I may have been dozing."

"I can call back later," she offered.

"No, this is a fine time. Have you found the jacket?"

"I haven't," Debbie said. "But I spoke with Jonathon Bell, and he'd like to come to Dennison Monday morning and interview you at eleven."

"About the jacket going missing?"

"Yes. He's hoping that publicity will help the case. We should probably check with Ian first, but if he says it's okay, would that be all right with you?"

"I suppose so." Ray paused a moment and then said, "Maybe we could do the interview outside the depot this time."

"I'm sure that would be fine. Monday is supposed to be a nice day."

"It would be good to include Elwood and Carl in the interview. We can show how sorry they are so people won't be suspicious that they took it. And you could ask Ian if he wants to give an official statement."

"Good idea," Debbie said. "I'll text Jonathon and tell him your suggestions."

"Hopefully the jacket will turn up before then."

"Yes, I hope so too," Debbie answered. "But if not, it would be good to get the word out that it's missing. Jonathon seems to think that if the thief sees a news story about it, they may be inspired to return it—maybe anonymously, but return it nonetheless."

"I hope that's true. Thank you for your help," Ray said.

"You're welcome. I'll be in touch with details about Monday."

Debbie texted Jonathon and then decided to stop by the dry cleaners once more. When she entered the shop, Ian was talking with Carl at the counter.

"Hey," Debbie said. "Am I interrupting anything?"

"No," Carl said. "Ian was telling me it'll be a few more days until he gets evidence back from the footprint analysis." He held up a photo of the shoe print.

"Is that to scale?" Debbie asked.

"Yes," Ian replied.

"Ian said it was overdeveloped to show the entire print." Carl handed the photo to Debbie.

She peered at it then at Ian. "Can you tell the size?"

Ian smiled. "I don't suppose it would hurt to tell you, since you were the one who discovered it in the first place. It's a men's size ten, and it's some sort of athletic shoe. I sent the information to the state lab to be analyzed. I should hear back from them by next week."

"I'm a size twelve." Carl stepped away from the counter so they could see. His shoes were obviously bigger than the image on the paper.

"Good to know," Debbie said. "How about Elwood? Do you know his shoe size?"

Carl tilted his head. "There's no way Elwood could climb that tree and get himself through the window. We're both of an age where that kind of activity is long behind us."

"You're not much older than I am," Ian said.

Carl patted his belly. "I'm afraid my situation is more shape than age."

Ian shrugged. "I've seen all sizes of people do all sorts of things. You'd be surprised." Then he added, "Of course, the print may not be from the thief. Maybe someone running by decided to make a steeplechase of the picnic table."

That could be a possibility. Perhaps knowing more details about the shoe wouldn't help. But perhaps it would.

"Do you have any new information?" Ian asked Debbie. "It's too much to hope that you've kept your nose out of this." He folded his arms across his chest.

Debbie felt her face get warm. "Jonathon Bell is coming back Monday morning to interview Ray again, this time about the missing jacket," she said. "He's hoping that getting the word out will inspire someone who knows something about it to come forward—or maybe scare the thief into returning the jacket. If all that is okay with you, that is."

"It's worth a try," Ian said.

"I'm glad you think so," Debbie said. "Ray also suggested that you might want to make an official statement?"

"I'll keep that as an option," Ian said.

"Oh, and Carl, Jonathon would like to interview you as well."

"Me?"

"Yes. And maybe Elwood too."

"Why?"

Debbie smiled. "Like Elwood said, you don't want people thinking that customers' items regularly go missing from your shop."

"That's true," Carl said. "But do we want to advertise that it went missing from our shop in the first place?"

"Ah." Debbie hadn't thought of that. "Good point."

"I'll talk it over with Elwood and get back to you."

After saying goodbye to Carl, Ian and Debbie left the shop. Once they were outside, Ian said, "I wonder what size shoe Jonathon Bell wears."

"You can ask him Monday morning," Debbie answered, "but there's no way he could climb through that window."

"True. How about his cameraman?"

"He's much younger. I'd put him in his thirties," Debbie mused. "And he wore athletic shoes. But I'm pretty sure he left with Jonathon. They had a high school graduation to get to. Or that's what Jonathon said anyway."

"What time is Jonathon doing the interview on Monday?" Ian asked.

"Eleven o'clock, outside the depot."

"Perfect," Ian said. "I'll be there."

After Debbie left the dry cleaners, she drove to Good Shepherd. She'd make sure the interview on Monday morning was on Ray's calendar.

When she arrived, she found Ray staring out the window of the common area onto the grounds of Good Shepherd.

"Penny for your thoughts," Debbie said.

Ray wheeled his chair around. "Hello, Debbie. I was thinking more about the war. About those days in Normandy. About Leland Clark and the Dumas family." He had a faraway look in his eyes. "About all of it."

CHAPTER NINE

Normandy, France
July 1, 1944

Sergeant Clark and Ray snuck out of line and knocked on Alié's back door as their platoon marched toward the Vire-et-Taute Canal, but no one opened the door. Ray guessed with so many troops on the move, the family had hunkered down, determined to protect the food they had left. He hoped the money they'd earned from selling some of what they had to his squad would help them return home once Paris was liberated.

As they hustled to rejoin their group, Ray glanced behind him. A figure was in the window, but he couldn't tell if it was Alié or Anne. He waved in case whoever it was could see him. Then he and Sergeant Clark fell back in line.

Ray's platoon traversed the countryside of fields, hedges, woods, and more hedges. The hedges were planted on high earthen walls, three feet and higher, which surrounded and enclosed the fields. Sergeant Clark said they dated back to Roman times and marked property lines. The men had to advance single file and then scale the earthen walls, which drew enemy gunfire and sometimes even fire from tanks.

Every time he crossed a hedge, Ray said a prayer and moved as quickly as he could. His company had helped drive the Germans to the other side of the canal, and now the next objective was crossing the canal and the Vire River and confronting them again.

As he ate his rations, Ray often thought wistfully of the roasted chickens Alié's family had sold to them. But even better than the food was being inside a home with a family, playing a piano while they sang. That moment of celebrating their common humanity through music had given him strength when he'd felt at his lowest. It had been the worst of birthdays—but also the best. He'd never take his family for granted again. He'd never take music for granted again. He'd never take anything for granted again.

With each step he felt his resolve and faith growing.

The troops waded across the three-foot deep canal. Halfway across, Clark fell up to his neck. He held

his rifle above his head and staggered a few steps. Ray
hurried to help him, taking the weapon so Clark could
find his footing.

After he did and took his rifle back, Ray pointed to
the shore. "Go ahead," he said. "I'll cover you."

"Thanks," Sergeant Clark said. Were his hands
shaking? He blinked a couple of times and continued.
Concern rose in Ray. Their leader had been so strong
and determined as they fought on Omaha Beach and
up into the hedgerows.

But everyone had a breaking point. Ray had certainly felt he was near it on his birthday. He'd do everything he could to help Sergeant Clark get past his.

Soon they were all on the other side. After they
dug foxholes and settled in, Ray grabbed his rifle and
asked Clark if he wanted to go hunt for birds to add
fresh meat to their boxed suppers.

Clark declined, so Ray went by himself. Each day
since his birthday, he'd grown less anxious and more
confident. He wasn't sure if that was a good thing or
not. He wasn't as cautious as he had been. He found
himself taking more risks. He didn't cross the line into
foolhardy, but he toed it more than he probably should.
He knew overconfident soldiers could get themselves
killed, but he was desperate to break out of the

monotony of boredom and terror that came with fighting in war.

He headed toward the river, picking up rocks as he walked along. After a few minutes he stopped and threw a rock into the brush. After the third throw, a flock of pheasants flew up. He shot multiple times, felling three of the birds. He retrieved them and headed back to the foxhole.

The others were thrilled to see that they'd have meat for supper, but Sergeant Clark hardly paid any attention to Ray. Instead, he lay down and put his helmet over his face.

Ray started a fire, and a couple of his buddies helped him pluck the birds and find sticks to roast them.

Clark woke up to help eat the birds, but then he wandered away. As Ray got ready for guard duty, he said a prayer for Sergeant Clark. They needed their leader to stay strong.

A few days later they crossed the Vire River on a bridge set up by engineers from another company. Two soldiers in front of them were picked off by snipers and fell into the river, but everyone in Ray's platoon managed to cross unharmed. The next day, Lieutenant Cohen was *shot by a German sniper. He took the bullet in his shoulder and was immediately sent to the aid station. Orders came in for their division to head toward Belgium.*

Clark seemed even more rattled. "They're either sending us to Germany or the Netherlands," he muttered to Ray.

"Hopefully the Netherlands," Ray answered, keeping his tone light.

Clark frowned. "It doesn't matter. The Germans are in both places."

That was true.

The next month was a blur of fighting as they pushed the Germans farther east. Every morning— whether he was on guard duty or had been able to catch a couple of hours of sleep in his foxhole—Ray faced the day with gratitude. And then a prayer for Sergeant Clark.

Those prayers were answered when trucks showed up in the middle of August to haul their division the rest of the way across France. Sergeant Clark became more his old self—optimistic and gregarious. It didn't hurt that village people along the way cheered the American soldiers along, offering them songs and even sometimes food and drink. Sergeant Clark especially responded to the pretty young women who blew them kisses.

Ray breathed a sigh of relief. Clark was back to his old self, they'd received replacements for the troops they'd lost, and they had a new leader—Lieutenant Hollingsworth. An officer with no combat experience, but he seemed like a good man. He'd understand the ropes soon enough.

Ray's division pressed on, chasing the Germans and taking soldiers into captivity as they surrendered or were caught. A few battles slowed the troops, but once those were won, they continued forward. Allied troops liberated Paris on August 25. Every Frenchman they encountered was delirious with joy. Ray began to believe that the rainbow Alié had sung about might exist after all. As Sergeant Clark shared the news, he seemed to be entirely his old self again.

On the first of September, the 30th Division became the first American troops to enter Belgium. Again, they were greeted as heroes. But eventually a lack of fuel forced the soldiers off the trucks and back to marching. Soon after, Sergeant Clark confirmed they were headed to the Netherlands.

Once they reached the border, battles and skirmishes continued, but nothing like they'd faced in France. Sergeant Clark was more energetic and charming than ever.

That ended the middle of September when they reached Valkenburg and the Geul River. The Germans were dug into trenches north of the river, and the

30th came under heavy artillery fire, the worst they'd faced in weeks. The screech of the artillery and the smell of smoke grated on Ray's nerves. They were unable to cross the river at first, and Sergeant Clark ordered the men to hunker down and wait.

Shortly after dusk fell, another platoon splashed into the water to cross the Geul. Enemy fire hit one soldier, and the others carried him the rest of the way. By the time they reached the other bank, it was too dark for Ray to see where they went.

More fire rained on them through the night. Sergeant Clark didn't sleep and became more and more agitated, pacing back and forth behind the platoon.

"Sarge," Ray finally said, "get down and try to rest. I'll keep watch."

Clark relented, and Ray took his place, crouching with a good view of the river, his helmet pulled low on his forehead.

One of the privates lit a cigarette, and an incoming mortar landed a few feet away.

"Put that out, Private," Ray ordered.

The private obeyed and stayed flat. Another mortar zipped past them, and Sergeant Clark gasped.

An hour later it seemed everyone had gone to sleep, but soon Sergeant Clark was up again. "We're sitting ducks here. I'm going to cross the river. I'll light a match when I've made it, and you come with the rest."

Ray didn't think that was a good idea but didn't say so. The sergeant was on edge. Challenging him would only make things worse, besides being insubordinate.

Clark ran to the bank and then splashed into the water. Gunfire erupted, and in between shots, Ray could hear him making his way across. There was a moment of silence and then another shot, followed by a scream of pain.

Ray slid down the bank and into the water. As he splashed forward, Sergeant Clark moaned. Ray slung his rifle over his shoulder and swung in that direction. After a moment, he bumped against something.

"My leg," Clark groaned.

Ray grabbed him and started dragging him back.

When they got there, Clark managed to crawl up the bank with Ray behind him.

Dawn was breaking when they reached the top. As Ray stood to help Clark, another shot rang out. And then another. Ray felt like a rock had slammed into his leg. Then something hit the back of his helmet, and he fell forward, knocking Sergeant Clark down too.

When Ray came to, a medic was holding smelling salts to his nose and Lieutenant Hollingsworth stood over him.

"I'm all right." Ray tried to sit up, but the medic gently pushed him back down.

"Actually, you're not," Hollingsworth said. "You've been shot, Zink. Your helmet saved your life, but you still got your noggin rung, not to mention the bullet in your leg."

Ray closed his eyes. "How's Sarge?"

"He's all right. He's been shot in the leg too."

The medic and a private transferred Ray onto a stretcher and headed toward a truck. Hollingsworth walked alongside Ray. "Thank you for your bravery in saving Clark. You'll get a Purple Heart out of your million-dollar wound. It's bad enough to get you out of the fighting for a while, but the medic says it's not fatal or crippling as long as nothing goes wrong with the recovery process."

Ray didn't relish being wounded or leaving the front. He felt he was letting the other soldiers down. But he knew his injury could work against him if it didn't heal properly, and his death would hurt his brothers-in-arms more than his temporary absence.

After Ray was loaded into the truck, he craned his neck to search for Clark. He found the sergeant sitting on a bench, his leg extended and his eyes closed. "How are you, Sarge?"

"All right," Clark said. "I didn't feel anything until I was in the water, but I must have been shot up on the bank."

They didn't talk after that as the truck headed west, toward Belgium and on to France. They crossed the channel on a ferry at Calais to England and arrived in Dover, where they were loaded and trucked to the North Somerset village of Wraxall and the 74th General Hospital. The Tyntesfield estate, a stately and expansive home along with a collection of tents and added buildings, housed the hospital.

The bullet that had torn through Ray's calf had nicked the bone but not shattered it. However, infection soon flared, and the wound had to be scrubbed several times. Ray also had a concussion from the bullet hitting his helmet and had headaches that lasted for weeks.

But many of the other soldiers had lost arms or legs, had stomach or chest wounds, or head and spine injuries. Ray counted his blessings. He hadn't wanted to be wounded. He'd wanted to keep serving with his platoon. But the cot, tea, three meals a day, and warm water to bathe were luxuries he'd dreamed about over the last three and a half months.

Sergeant Clark's leg needed surgery, and he made many friends at the hospital, including a British nurse,

Edith Burns. Ray wasn't surprised. Clark had been back to his usual outgoing self once they were on the truck headed west. He'd only grown more so when they reached England. Away from the front, the war seemed like a grand adventure for him again.

Ray couldn't fault him. They'd both thought Omaha Beach would be the worst they'd see in Europe. Instead, it had only been the beginning of a long and terrifying nightmare.

A couple of weeks later, Ray and Clark sat out in the warm sunshine.

"Where do you think the 30th is now?" Ray asked.

"I have no idea." Sergeant Clark lay back on the grass. "And I don't care."

Ray didn't believe him. "How long do you think until they send us back?"

"They might use us to fill another division." Clark used his crutches to stand up. "Hopefully one going home."

Ray chuckled. "We're not going home. We'll be walking soon." They'd heard the liberation of the Netherlands wasn't going as quickly as everyone had hoped, and the Allies were bogged down. Others made their way across France but hadn't reached Germany yet. Ray expected they'd both be sent back to their platoon.

There was a piano in the mess hall, and one day someone was picking out a tune when Sergeant Clark belted out, "We have a professional piano player right here, don't we, Specialist Zink?"

Ray's face grew warm.

"I hope I'm not being rude," Clark said to the man who stood and moved away from the bench.

"Not at all," the man said. "I'd love to listen to someone who can really play.'

"Go on," Sergeant Clark said to Ray.

Ray stood and, with the help of his crutches, made his way to the bench. He sat down and placed his hands on the keys. The piano wasn't as nice as the one at the Dumas home, but it would do.

Ray knew he wanted to play something upbeat. He ran a few scales to make sure the piano was in tune then launched into "Chattanooga Choo Choo." By the time he was a few lines in, people began singing along to the familiar tune.

He played the song with gusto until the final chord. The crowd cheered. Someone called, "More!"

Ray began "God Save the King." The Brits immediately stood and sang along.

When Ray finished the last note, before he could start another song, someone began singing in a loud and clear voice, "Oh, say can you see..." Ray found the key, played along, and others joined in the singing.

At the end of the anthem, Ray played crashing chords in a rousing finish and then stood and pushed the bench in.

Someone yelled, "More!"

Sergeant Clark held up his hands. "Tomorrow. Same time, same place."

Grateful to Clark, Ray said, "Bring requests."

After that, Ray played every day during the noon meal, and other patients and the staff began to recognize him. When she could, Edith would come and sit with Sergeant Clark and listen to Ray play.

By the end of August, Sergeant Clark and Ray had healed, and the doctor released them, although both still walked with a bit of a limp. Instead of receiving orders to go back to the 30th, they were attached to a bomb-disposal team working with the British Royal Engineers. Sergeant Clark was thrilled. "That'll be a piece of cake."

Ray wasn't so sure. It sounded like work that would require a lot of precision and care.

"Besides," Sergeant Clark said, "I'll be fairly close to Edith and hopefully able to see her from time to time."

They began on the southern coast in Poldhu, Cornwall. British beaches had been mined by engineers in 1940 when the British anticipated a German invasion. Beginning in 1943, once it seemed that was no longer a possibility, engineers began removing the mines. All in all, there were about 2,000 minefields and nearly 350,000 mines. A lot of work had to be done before the British were safe to return to their beaches.

A young woman who worked as a secretary for the Royal Engineers was at the Poldhu compound. Her name was Izzy, and Sergeant Clark became acquainted with her right away. One day when Ray went to check his mail, still hoping for a letter from Eleanor, a boy around six was in the office with her, sitting in a chair beside her desk. He wore short pants and a jacket and had a head of thick red hair. Izzy didn't seem old enough to have a child, but perhaps she was.

"Ray," she said, "I'd like to introduce you to my brother, Timmy."

Ray extended his hand. "Nice to meet you, Timmy. Are you visiting Izzy?"

"No, we live here now in a boardinghouse. Ever since Bodmin was bombed."

"Our landlady had an appointment this afternoon," Izzy said. "She usually watches Timmy."

"Our mum and dad were killed in the bombing, but I wasn't hurt." Timmy sounded matter-of-fact, which was perhaps not uncommon for a child who had gone through such a tragedy.

Ray knelt in front of Timmy. "I'm so sorry to hear about your parents."

"It's all right. It's not your fault." Timmy squared his shoulders. "I wish you American soldiers had come sooner though."

"So do I," Ray said.

Sergeant Clark came into the office with a big smile for Izzy. "There's a movie tonight. Want to go with me?"

Izzy smiled and gestured to her brother.

"Hello, Timmy," Sergeant Clark said. "Nice to see you." Ray wondered when Sergeant Clark had met Timmy. Perhaps he'd been to the boardinghouse to visit Izzy.

Later that evening when they were back in their barracks, Sergeant Clark said to Ray, "Edith is dating other people too. It's not as if we're exclusive or anything."

"I didn't say anything," Ray said.

Sergeant Clark squinted at him. "But did you think it?"

"No. Who you date is your business," Ray replied.

Around Christmas, Clark managed to secure orders for himself and Ray to return to Wraxall. They attended services on Christmas Eve in the chapel with Edith and then started making their way to a gathering in the mess hall. As Ray followed Sergeant Clark and Edith across the grounds, he caught sight of an old man with a shock of white hair standing outside the women's ward.

"Grand-Oncle!" he called out.

Sergeant Clark turned to Ray, but Ray didn't take time to explain. He began hurrying across the field toward the man, guessing that Alié or Anne or Madame Dumas had been injured. Or perhaps all three.

CHAPTER TEN

*A*s Debbie put on her makeup the next morning before church, her phone buzzed. It was Betsy, Reed's mom. Debbie hadn't seen her late fiancé's mother since December, although they'd spoken a few times on the phone.

She accepted the call. "Hi, Betsy. How are you?"

"Just fine, sweetie. How are you? How's the café doing?"

"Really well, both the café and me. It's our busy season. We're getting lots of tourists, along with more locals, since school is out."

"How nice," Betsy said.

Debbie put her mascara wand back in the tube. "How is June in Florida?"

"Getting hot," Betsy said. "Listen, I'm going to get right to it. I had an interesting message this morning from a soldier who served with Reed. He didn't know your last name, so he called me."

"I see," Debbie said, wondering where this was going.

"Would it be all right if I give you his number so you can reach out to him?"

"Sure," Debbie replied. "Do you know what this is about?"

"I have no idea, actually," Betsy said. "All I know is that he wants to talk to you."

Debbie couldn't think of what to say.

"Are you all right, dear?" Betsy asked.

"I'm think I'm in a bit of shock," Debbie said. "It's been so long. Twenty years."

"I know," Betsy said. "And that visit we had last December felt like the closure I needed, only to be surprised by this message. It's from a Thom—with an *h*—Matson."

Debbie didn't remember Reed mentioning anyone by that name.

"It brings it all back, doesn't it?" Betsy said in a low voice.

"Yes." Debbie realized she was whispering too. "At least for the moment," she said in a normal tone. "How are you doing?"

"Really well," Betsy said. "There are bound to be moments like this, of course, but I'm happy. Life is good for the most part."

"I agree," Debbie said.

"Tell me how things are going for you. How is Greg?"

"Great," Debbie answered. "We officially started dating last month. He's busy with his boys, but we're making time for us too."

"That's wonderful," Betsy said. "I'm so happy for you."

"How are the wedding plans coming along?" Betsy had gotten engaged right before Debbie had last seen her.

"Good. We set a date for November, right after Thanksgiving. It will be a small gathering down in Key West."

"That sounds lovely," Debbie said.

Betsy laughed. "It will be. I can't tell you how happy I am." Her voice grew serious again. "You don't have to contact Thom. I don't want his request to interfere with your life. I told him I'd let you know but I couldn't promise him anything. No one will hold it against you, not even Thom."

"Thank you," Debbie said. "I'll think about it. Any chance you'll be up this way for a visit soon?"

"As a matter of fact, I may be in the area in the next week or so. I have some business to finish up from the sale of a property in Akron," Betsy said.

Debbie knew Betsy had a few rental houses that an uncle had left her. "Let me know. I'd love to see you if you have time."

"I will," Betsy answered. "In the meantime, I'll text you Thom's information."

"Thank you."

As Debbie ended the call, her stomach rolled with nerves. The sensation worsened when Betsy's text came through, sharing Thom's number.

What in the world could someone who had served with Reed want from her twenty years later?

Debbie thought of Reed all through church as she sat by Greg. She barely listened to Pastor Nick's sermon, noting the scripture was Matthew 5:4, "Blessed are those who mourn, for they will be comforted."

She'd finally worked through her grief for Reed. Betsy's phone call hadn't brought it back. Not the heartbreaking grief she'd felt when she first found out Reed had been killed. Not the life-shattering aftermath. Not even the final layer she'd peeled off months ago.

She was once again experiencing the dull, underlying ache that she'd lived with for so long.

Greg shifted a little, and his leg pressed against hers. Meeting Greg and spending time with him—someone who had experienced the grief of losing his wife—and now dating him had made that ache go away.

Should she contact Thom Matson? What if what he had to tell her was disturbing?

She didn't want to tear the scab off of her grief. No, it wouldn't be like that. It would be more like cutting into scar tissue.

Pastor Nick said, "Let us pray," and Debbie realized she'd missed most of the sermon. After Reed died, it had been difficult to go to church. She'd find herself lost deep in thought about Reed, and she'd go home feeling exhausted.

Greg leaned toward her. "Are you okay?"

She smiled at him. "Yes."

Pastor Nick said, "Please stand," and the pianist began playing, "To God Be the Glory."

Debbie absolutely knew God had done great things as the hymn proclaimed. Despite Reed's death. Despite the years of grief she'd worked through. Despite a soldier who'd known Reed wanting to talk with her out of the blue.

After church, Greg walked Debbie to her car. They crossed the church lawn, where Jaxon and Julian chatted with other kids from the church youth group under the shadow of the steeple.

"What do you and the boys have planned for this afternoon?" Debbie asked.

"Lunch at Mom's. Are you off to your parents' house?"

Debbie nodded.

When they reached her car, Greg said, "You seemed distracted during the service."

"I guess I was."

"Want to talk about it?"

She hesitated and then said, "I had a call from Reed's mom right before I left for church. She said one of Reed's soldier buddies contacted her. He wants to talk to me."

"What about?"

"I don't know. Betsy gave me his contact information." Debbie shaded her eyes. The day had grown warm. "I'm supposed to contact him if I want to talk to him."

"Do you want to?" Greg asked.

"I'm not sure. It's been twenty years. I don't—" She dropped her hand.

Greg put his hand on her shoulder. "You don't want to feel everything all over again?"

"I don't think I would. No matter what he says." She met Greg's eyes. He'd lost his wife to cancer. He knew grief. "I can't imagine that what he'd have to say would have an impact on how I feel about Reed or my grief or what I've worked through. But the thought of talking to him is making me anxious."

"Maybe what this soldier has to say has more to do with himself than Reed."

She hadn't thought of that. "Maybe."

"Whatever the reason, consider the bond Ray had with Leland Clark. I imagine Reed had those same kind of connections with the men he served with."

"That could be true." Debbie gave him a small smile. "I hadn't thought of that. Maybe I'll text him this afternoon."

When Debbie arrived at her parents' place on the outskirts of town, where she'd grown up, they hadn't arrived from church yet. She parked in the driveway, leaving plenty of room for their vehicle, and then walked to the back door and let herself in. The kitchen smelled like pot roast, the aroma making her mouth water. A bowl of strawberries sat on the counter along with homemade shortcakes still on the cooling rack.

She stepped into the dining room. The table was set for three with the good china. Often, Mom and Dad invited others for Sunday dinner. Debbie was glad it would be just the three of them today. She needed to talk to them and get their advice and support.

Her parents had always been there for her, in the past and in the present. She was grateful they were active and in good shape.

A car door slammed and then another. And then a third. Had they brought someone home with them? Debbie's heart sank. She'd wanted to talk with them about Thom Matson.

She stepped through the kitchen to the porch, wondering who they would have brought home with them. She opened the door, ready to be friendly and gracious.

But it was just her dad and her mom—who was carrying a laundry basket of dish towels and tablecloths from the church. That third slam must have been when she pulled them from the back seat.

Debbie chuckled.

"What's so funny?" Mom asked.

"Nothing," Debbie said. "I'm just really happy to see you."

After dinner, they took their iced coffee and strawberry short-cake with whipped cream out to the patio. After she admired Dad's strawberry patch beside his expansive garden, Debbie told them that a soldier who had served with Greg wanted to speak with her.

"Do you want to talk to him now?" Dad asked. "While we're with you?"

She hadn't thought about having someone with her. "I appreciate that, but it's not necessary." She glanced from her father to her mother. "But you think I should contact him?"

Mom hesitated then said, "You could give it a try. If it doesn't seem to be a good situation, you could always hang up."

Debbie considered this. "But it's been so long," she said after a moment.

"Which means this man has been holding on to something for twenty years," Mom said. "And it took him that long to work up the nerve to contact you."

"You have a point." Debbie took a bite of her dessert. Nothing tasted as much like summer as strawberry shortcake.

When Debbie got home, she took out her phone and retrieved Thom Matson's contact information. And then she stared at her phone. *Twenty years.* What could he possibly have to say to her?

Whatever what it was, Debbie hoped she could respond in an appropriate way. And as Mom advised, she could end the call if the conversation didn't go well.

Her phone rang, making her jump. It was Ray.

Relieved, she answered the phone. "Hi, Ray. How are you this afternoon?"

"I can't complain," he said. "I didn't go to church this morning. I felt a little tired."

"Then it's good that you rested."

"Any word about the jacket?"

"Not yet," Debbie said.

"So we're still on as far as the interview tomorrow?"

"Yes. I'll confirm with Jonathon and pick you up at ten thirty."

"All right." Ray paused. Then he said, "I keep thinking about Leland Clark and what we went through together. It meant a lot to meet Heather and Ruby. I felt a connection with them because of Leland. War does funny things to people."

"I can only imagine," Debbie said. "Do you have time for me to ask your advice about something?"

"Of course. I always have time to give advice." He chuckled. "And I always have time for you."

"I don't take a second of that for granted." She took a deep breath and said, "Do you remember my fiancé, Reed, who was killed in Afghanistan?"

"Do I remember? I prayed for him after he was captured. And for you too. We were all devastated when we found out he'd been killed. I felt a connection with you because of those prayers. But also because you'd been touched by war too. We have that in common."

"Thank you," Debbie said. "I had no idea you followed Reed's story and mine while it was happening."

"The whole town did," Ray said. "Your parents asked for prayer, and everyone prayed."

"I felt those prayers." They hadn't changed the outcome, but they had changed her. She'd trusted God through the worst ordeal of her life, and He had faithfully brought her through it.

"Eileen and I went to the burial for Reed together. Kim drove us. We stayed in the back, close to Kim's car. But we were there."

"Oh, I had no idea," Debbie said. "Thank you."

"It was the least we could do." Ray's voice was soft. "What do you need advice about?"

"A soldier who served with Reed wants to talk to me. I don't know what about, and I'm feeling apprehensive about it. What do you think I should do?"

"Well, even if it's a stretch for you, I think it would be a good idea to at least listen to what he has to say. If for any reason you don't feel comfortable with the conversation or the direction it's taking, tell him that. Have you considered meeting with him in person?"

"No," Debbie said. "I don't know where he lives or if it would be an option to meet in person."

"Find out," Ray said. "That kind of conversation is always better in person."

The sense of Ray's words hit her. What he said felt right. "That's true. Thank you."

After saying goodbye to Ray, Debbie composed a text to Thom Matson before she lost her nerve. HI, THOM. THIS IS DEBBIE ALBRIGHT. BETSY BRANDT GAVE ME YOUR NUMBER AND SAID YOU WANTED TO SPEAK WITH ME. I WAS WONDERING WHERE YOU LIVE AND IF WE MIGHT MEET IN PERSON.

A text came back immediately. THANK YOU FOR RESPONDING TO MY REQUEST. I'M STAYING IN COLUMBUS. ARE YOU STILL IN CLEVELAND?

No. I live in Dennison now.

Could I come see you on Tuesday around one? Let me know a good place to meet.

Ray's advice had worked. Why not meet at the café? A public place she was comfortable in, with Janet nearby, would be the perfect option. She texted him back with the details.

CHAPTER ELEVEN

The next morning, when Debbie and Ray arrived at the Dennison Depot right before eleven, the newsroom van wasn't anywhere in sight. Had Jonathon changed his mind? Debbie had left a message to confirm the evening before but hadn't heard back from him.

Maybe another big story had come up. She checked her phone. She hadn't missed a message from Jonathon. But she did have one from Ian saying he wouldn't make the interview and that he'd let Jonathon know.

As she got Ray's wheelchair out of her car, Carl and Elwood walked around the corner of the depot. They spotted her and hurried to help her transfer Ray to the chair.

"Thank you," Debbie said. "Who's watching the shop?"

"Sylvie," Elwood said. "Although she'd rather be here. We've been watching Jonathon Bell for years. He's always been one of her favorites."

Ray shook both men's hands in greeting. "Thank you again for helping us."

"I can't tell you how sick we are about your jacket," Elwood told him. "We've never had anything like this happen before."

"I don't blame either of you," Ray said.

"Well, you should. Something must have been wrong with our security."

Ray shrugged. "Things happen."

"We really hope someone can figure this out," Carl said. "Or that the thief returns it unharmed."

"Yes," Ray said. "That's my prayer as well."

Elwood laid his hand on Carl's shoulder. "We decided the best thing to do is be honest about what happened. We don't want to appear to be hiding anything. And we want everyone to know that we're investigating the hole in our security and will fix it as soon as we can."

The moment was interrupted by Jonathon shouting out of the news van window. "We're here!"

As Jonathon and his cameraman unloaded their equipment, Janet came out of the depot and made her way to Debbie's side. "Paulette is keeping an eye on the café. I thought I'd see how things were going out here."

"Good, I think." Debbie dropped her voice to a whisper. "What size shoe do you think Jonathon wears?"

"Bigger than a ten," Janet whispered back. "I overheard Ian on the phone about the size of the footprint." She nodded toward the cameraman's shoes, which were light hikers. "His are at least twelves."

Debbie agreed.

A few minutes later, Jonathon began the interview with Ray. The two sat at a patio table against the brick exterior wall of the depot. Jonathon asked Ray about the missing jacket, why it had been at the dry cleaners, and how he'd found out it was gone.

Then he stood and interviewed Carl. "Do you think it's likely the jacket will be found?"

"Our police department is doing their best," Carl said.

"Any suspects?" Jonathon asked.

"The police haven't announced any suspects yet," Carl responded. "But we're hoping the thief will see this report and feel compelled to return the jacket." He looked straight into the camera. "Please return it to the dry cleaners or the Dennison police station. No questions asked. We just want it back. Ray Zink needs his World War II jacket returned."

Jonathon wrapped up the segment by addressing the camera. "There you have it. A World War II hero and his missing army jacket need to be reunited. If you can help make that happen, contact me at the newsroom or contact the Dennison Police Department." He paused a moment and then said, "I try not to get too personal with my reports, but I've had a lifelong interest in World War II and have met more heroes than I can count. And I have to say, Ray Zink is one of the most remarkable. He was injured both in the Netherlands during the war and on Guernsey, an island in the English Channel, while clearing mines there. He was a brave soldier—and I assume every bit as humble as he is now. Let's get this man's jacket back to him."

The cameraman said, "That's a wrap."

"Nice." Janet squeezed Debbie's hand. "I'm going to work. See you soon." She hurried into the depot.

Jonathon shook Ray's hand. "Let's hope this segment will help. It's good to see you again, but I'm sorry about the circumstances."

"Thank you for your help," Ray said.

Jonathon started toward the van as Carl sat down at the table with Ray and struck up a conversation.

Debbie followed the newscaster. "Do you have to rush off? I have a couple of questions."

"Walk with me," he said.

"I want to do some research on a friend's grandfather who was killed in March of 1943 in Tunisia. Have you done any research on soldiers? Do you have any recommendations for where I should start?"

"What do you want to find out?" he asked.

"How he died. And why he was awarded the Bronze Star."

"In that case, start with the National Archives. Everything is digitized now. You can also email them with questions or go in person. The morning reports or something else should provide the information you need."

"Morning reports?"

He shifted his microphone bag higher on his shoulder. "Those were reports that were written up every morning by the unit clerk. They detailed any changes in a soldier's status, like if they were transferred, assigned another duty, wounded, promoted. That kind of thing."

"And the National Archives has these reports?"

"They do."

"Thank you," Debbie said, "I really appreciate it."

"You're welcome." He gave her his megawatt smile. "Have a good day."

They'd reached the van, and the cameraman was loading his gear in the back. Jonathon reached for the driver's door handle.

"I have one more question," Debbie said.

Jonathon turned toward her.

"I noticed that you didn't mention that Ray saved a little girl's life on Guernsey. Was there a reason for that?"

"Well, that hasn't been confirmed, right? Heather Clark is adamant that her father saved that girl. She called me on Friday to hash it all out again. Leland Clark mentioned many times that he saved a girl. Ray didn't say anything until Oliver Godfrey came along."

"Well, that's Ray's nature. He's not going to brag about himself."

Jonathon shrugged. "Godfrey's mother might have been confused about the name. Maybe once Ray was injured, his was the name that stuck."

"Or Ray did rescue the girl, and that's why she remembered his name."

"Yes, that's a possibility. But I don't have confirmation either way, and I don't have any evidence of Ray talking about the rescue through the years like Leland did. I'm not going to put it on the air when I don't know for sure which one did it." He glanced at his watch. "I've got to get going. It was a bit of a squeeze to fit this in today."

Debbie waved. "We appreciate it. Thank you."

"It'll be on the six o'clock news." He climbed into the driver's seat as the cameraman got into the passenger side. "Let me know when the jacket turns up."

Debbie stepped away from the vehicle. "I will."

Before Janet left for the day, she and Debbie sat down at a table with cups of coffee to go over the rest of the week.

"Tiffany's coming home this evening," Janet said. "I was hoping to take off early tomorrow and spend some time with her."

Tiffany was Janet and Ian's nineteen-year-old daughter who had finished her first year at Case Western Reserve University in Cleveland a month ago. She had gone back to Cleveland for a few days to see friends and interview for a part-time job at the college that would begin in August, once school started. Until then, she'd keep working in Dennison as a lifeguard.

Debbie leaned back in her chair. "Uh-oh."

"What's up?"

"I forgot to tell you." She explained about Thom Matson coming the next afternoon to visit with her.

"Paulette will be here, right?"

"She's leaving at noon for a doctor's appointment."

"All right," Janet said. "I'll stay until closing. You might need me."

"What about Tiffany?"

"I'll see if she wants to hang out here tomorrow afternoon and maybe pitch in. What about Wednesday? Do you have anything going on then?"

"Nothing," Debbie said. "I'll be here all day."

"Great. I'll leave early to spend some time with her that afternoon. She's working in the morning at the pool, both tomorrow and Wednesday. Any progress on Ray's jacket that couldn't be shared in the interview?"

Debbie shook her head. "Hopefully Jonathon's segment about it will get someone's attention."

"What about Oliver Godfrey?"

"Nothing," Debbie answered. "I emailed the Isle of Guernsey Society office about him but haven't gotten a response. I'll contact their local law enforcement tomorrow if I don't hear back by then."

"Carl and Elwood are off the hook?"

"It's unlikely they took the jacket, but I don't know that anyone is off the hook."

"Including Jonathon Bell?"

"I'd say he's still on the list. I need to look into him more."

"I'll do some sleuthing tonight," Janet said. "I thought of something during the interview that might help. The mom of one of Tiffany's friends used to work with Jonathon at the station years ago. Her name is Cassie Howell. She moved back to Columbus last summer and has been doing some consulting work there." Janet held up her phone. "I happen to have her number. I'll see if she can give us any information on Jonathon."

"Great." Debbie took a last drink of coffee and rose to her feet. "You should get going. I'm guessing you have a lot to do before Tiffany gets home. I'll handle cleanup."

"I really don't have much except cooking dinner. I'm making pasta primavera and key lime pie for dinner."

"Yum."

"Do you want to come over?"

"That's tempting, but I need to get some things done." She had a thought and grabbed Janet's arm. "Wait. Did Tiffany get the part-time job?"

Janet smiled. "She did."

"That's wonderful. What is it exactly?"

"Working in the PR department for the college. It should be a great experience."

Debbie grimaced. "You wanted to celebrate with her tomorrow, didn't you?"

Janet shook her head as she too stood up. "It's fine. We'll celebrate Wednesday." She hugged Debbie. "I'll see you in the morning."

An hour later, Debbie finished cleaning the café, boxed a strawberry scone with white chocolate drizzled over the top, and then headed to the museum. It was closed on Mondays, but Kim had stopped in the café for a cup of coffee earlier and said she was going to spend a couple of hours catching up on paperwork.

Debbie called her as she walked through the lobby of the depot. "Mind if I stop by for a few minutes? I have a question."

"Why am I not surprised?" Kim laughed. "I'm headed to the door, so I'll let you in."

When Kim opened the door, Debbie handed her the boxed pastry. "Here's my payment."

Kim took the box and opened it. "Strawberry. Yum." She smiled at Debbie. "What do you need?"

"Resources on World War II soldiers. Greg's grandfather, Earl Connor Sr., in particular."

Kim led the way to her office. "Come on in." She settled into the chair behind her desk while Debbie sat in the visitor's chair in front of it. "What information do you have on him?"

"He died in March of 1943 in the Battle of El Guettar and was awarded a Purple Heart and a Bronze Star. I spoke with Jonathon Bell about researching him, and he said I should start with the National Archives."

"What do you want to find out?"

"Why exactly he was awarded the Bronze Star, the circumstances of his death, and where he was buried, if possible."

"They don't know where he was buried?"

"Greg doesn't," Debbie explained. "I would guess his grandmother knew, but she died when he was a kid."

Kim turned to her computer. "There are a few different places to look. Where he's buried should be pretty easy. I'll see if I can find that now." She clicked the mouse and then typed something. "As far as the reason for the Bronze Star and how he died, that might be a little harder."

After staring at the screen a moment and clicking again, she asked, "What's his full name?"

"Earl Gregory Connor Sr. He was born in 1917 and he died—" She pulled up the information on her phone, where she'd saved a photo of his obituary. "March 23, 1943. He served with the 1st Infantry Division."

Kim typed and scrolled for a couple of minutes. Then she said, "He's buried in the North Africa American Cemetery, in Tunis, Tunisia, along with over twenty-eight hundred other American soldiers."

"Thank you," Debbie said, typing the information in a note on her phone.

"As far as the other information, you can check the National Archives website. Have Greg follow the directions to request copies of the morning reports from the day his grandfather died plus a couple of days before and after. I'll email you the link, along with instructions on getting the most out of your search." Kim met Debbie's gaze. "Chances are you'll be able to get the information you need."

In the evening, Debbie ate dinner and watched Jonathon's interview with Ray on the six o'clock news.

She was tending the roses that Ray's mother had planted after the war when her phone buzzed with a text from Greg. WANT TO WALK HAMMER WITH ME? THE BOYS ARE WATCHING ANOTHER WWII MOVIE, AND I'M GETTING A LITTLE BURNED-OUT ON THOSE.

I'D LOVE TO, she texted back.

Twenty minutes later, Debbie was watering the forget-me-nots Ray had planted in the front yard as Greg and Hammer came around the corner. The dog gave a happy bark, and Greg waved.

Debbie turned off the water and met Greg on the sidewalk for a hug. They strolled toward the depot, chatting about their days.

Debbie told him that Kim had discovered his grandfather was buried in the North Africa American Cemetery. "I went on the website after work. There's a contact button, so maybe you could request a photograph of his gravesite."

"That's a good idea," Greg said. "Thank you. Did Kim have any ideas for next steps?"

"You bet." Debbie told him about Jonathon's and Kim's advice to research his grandfather's time of service further.

"Thank you for your help."

"I'll forward you the information Kim sent me."

A squirrel scurried across the street, and Hammer tugged at the end of the leash.

Ahead, Harry sat in a chair on his lawn with Crosby at his feet.

Debbie called out a greeting, and then they stopped and chatted for a few minutes before continuing on their way again.

As they headed back to Debbie's house, Greg asked, "What did you decide to do about the soldier who served with Reed?"

"I decided to talk with him. He's coming to the café tomorrow afternoon."

"He lives nearby?"

"He's been staying in Columbus. He said he'd drive down."

Greg smiled at her. "I'll be praying the meeting goes well. Let me know."

"I will."

They reached her house, and Greg gave her a hug. "Thank you for what you found out so far about my grandfather. I appreciate it."

"You're welcome." She squeezed his arm. "I'm excited to see what else you find out."

"Me too."

The next morning as they prepared to open the café, Janet reported that she'd heard back from the acquaintance who had worked with Jonathon Bell. "Cassie said he can sometimes be a little over-the-top and self-absorbed, but she's never known him to do anything dishonest or unprofessional. Beyond occasionally showing up late for an event or making a last-minute decision that a producer didn't like, anyway."

"Did she say anything about his World War II memorabilia collecting?"

"It's no secret. Everyone knows it's a hobby of his," Janet answered. "She doesn't think he has anything to hide. She said he even sells some of what he collects online."

"Really? Did she say where?"

Janet shook her head. "I should have asked. I'll send her another text."

As Debbie took orders, made drinks, and served food, she thought about Thom Matson. She'd researched him online on Sunday but hadn't found anything. Not even any social media pages. What if he wasn't who he said he was?

Paulette left at noon, and Debbie hustled to serve customers and clear tables. Maybe she should have asked Thom to come later than one, but then she risked Janet going home before she finished with him. She definitely didn't want to be alone in the café with Thom. Or maybe she should have asked her parents to come. They could have been on hand in case she needed them.

At twelve thirty Tiffany arrived to help. She gave Debbie a hug, checked in with her mom, and then got right to work.

At one there were two tables of customers left. Both had been served and were nearly done. Tiffany was in the kitchen with Janet.

At one forty-five, Thom Matson still hadn't arrived and Debbie had pretty much cleaned the dining room. Perhaps he wasn't coming.

But a minute later a man who appeared to be in his early forties with a completely bald head and dark brown eyes stepped through the door and locked eyes with her. "Debbie?"

"Yes."

"I'm Thom. Sorry I'm late."

CHAPTER TWELVE

*A*s Debbie handed Thom a cup of coffee and then sat down across from him, she wondered why she'd been so worried about meeting him. He had the respectful demeanor of a military professional and a warmth she hadn't expected.

Janet stepped to the counter and gave Debbie a questioning look. In response, Debbie raised her mug to her mouth with both hands and gave her a subtle thumbs-up.

If Thom noticed the exchange, he didn't act like it. "Thank you for meeting with me." He took a sip of coffee. "I can't believe it's taken me twenty years to contact you."

Debbie tilted her head and met his eyes but didn't say anything.

"At first, I was too broken to even think about talking with you. Then, about ten years ago, after a lot of healing, I started having this nagging feeling that I should. I tried to ignore it. I told myself it would only hurt you if I came out of the woodwork. You'd think I was crazy to reach out after so much time had passed. So the years kept slipping away from me."

"What changed?" Debbie asked.

"I've been helping my grandmother in Columbus for a few weeks. Last Sunday, in church with her, I had that nagging feeling again, that nudge. I had no idea how to find you because I didn't know your last name, but I promised myself I'd reach out to Reed's mother before the week was over. I waited until the last minute. But on Saturday, I did some digging, found Betsy Brandt, and sent her a message, praying that she'd tell me to drop the whole thing. That you wouldn't want to hear from me."

Debbie smiled.

"But you did."

She nodded. "I'm curious."

"No doubt." Thom leaned forward. "I want you to know what a remarkable man Reed was and what he did for all of us. Especially for me."

Debbie's heart skipped a beat. "Please tell me whatever you want to—whatever you need to. I've gone through a lot of healing over the years too."

"I'm glad to hear it. I'll tell you what I can." Thom took a deep breath as if to brace himself. "I know you heard from the army as events unfolded, starting with when Reed was captured."

"His parents did, since Reed and I weren't married yet. They shared what they were told with me."

"Which was?"

"That Reed defended his troops gallantly but was captured at the end of a skirmish. After he was killed, two soldiers came to their door."

Thom nodded. "The death notification."

"That's right."

"I was in Walter Reed by then. I was injured in the skirmish." He shook his head. "Is it all right if I start at the beginning?"

"I think that would be best."

"We were training Afghan border police in the Paktika province, on the border with Pakistan. Lots of Taliban fled after the invasion, but they were constantly firing missiles and coming over the border to attack the Afghan police, Afghan army, and us."

Debbie wrapped her hands tighter around her mug.

"We were on our way to the next village where Captain Brandt was going to meet with the elders and the Afghan police. Outside the village, fifty or sixty enemy soldiers surprised us. We hunkered down as Captain Brandt shouted commands to us and the Afghan police. The Taliban were positioned on both sides of the road and began shooting rocket-propelled grenades and then mortars. We moved our vehicles into a circle and managed to take cover except for a vehicle at the end of our convoy that was disabled by mortars. Reed ran back to it twice to pull injured soldiers into our circle."

Betsy had relayed that information to Debbie but not in as much detail.

"Reed requested air support, but it took hours for them to get there. All was quiet after they were finally able to leave, and we thought we'd be able to retreat, but as we ran to move the vehicles back into line to return to base, another wave of enemy fighters came charging from the hills. A bunch of us, including me, another private, and Captain Brandt hadn't made it to our vehicle yet."

Debbie took a sip of coffee and watched Janet turn the door sign to Closed.

"Enemy fighters swarmed down the hill. Captain Brandt told the private to get in the driver's seat, and that's when I took three bullets—one in the chest, one in the stomach, and one in the thigh.

I thought that was it for me. Captain Brandt yanked me up and shoved me in the vehicle and yelled, 'Drive!' The private stepped on it, and then he looked in the rearview mirror and said, 'Captain has his hands up.' I'll never forget his tone."

That, Debbie hadn't heard.

"He surrendered to save us. The enemy was so happy to have captured an officer that they called off the attack. We escaped. Captain Brandt gave his life for all of us, but for me in particular. He literally gave his life to save mine."

Debbie swallowed hard. "Thank you for sharing that. But why did you want to tell me instead of Reed's parents?"

"He told me once that if he died in action not to give his parents the details. To let them get the death notice and leave it at that. He thought it would be too hard on them. But he never told me that about you." Thom leaned back in his chair. "So why did it take me so long to find you? Because that's not all I wanted to tell you." He glanced down at his left hand, which sported a ring on the fourth finger.

Janet and Tiffany paused beside the table. "Hey, Debbie. We're ready to head out," Janet said. "Are you okay?"

"I'm okay." Debbie nodded to Thom. "This is Thom Matson. He served with Reed in Afghanistan. Thom, this is Janet Shaw and her daughter, Tiffany. Janet and I co-own the café together."

Thom stood and shook Janet's hand and then Tiffany's. "I'm pleased to meet you both."

"Pleased to meet you," Janet said. "Enjoy your time in Dennison. See you in the morning, Debbie. Call me if you need anything."

After Janet and Tiffany left, Thom asked Debbie, "Where were we?"

Debbie pointed at his ring.

"That's right. There are two other things I need to tell you. First of all, Captain Brandt was always open about his faith. I don't mean he preached at us or anything like that. But we knew he prayed, and we knew he trusted God with whatever happened. My grandmother used to take me to church. And like I said before, I still go with her when I visit."

Debbie smiled and waited for him to continue.

"Anyway, I made a commitment to God as a child but drifted away as I got older. The way Captain Brandt talked about God and the way he treated us made me want to find my way back."

"That was Reed," Debbie said. It had been one of the things she'd loved most about him.

"The second thing that impacted me was that he spoke about you with such respect and love. I grew up in a family where I didn't hear that, except from my grandmother. And I certainly didn't hear it from my buddies in the army. Captain Brandt was a few years older than most of us and set a better example. He made me want to get married someday, to love someone the way he loved you." He met her gaze. "I'm so sorry that never happened for you."

Debbie pointed to Thom's finger. "But it did happen for you, right? Tell me your story. What happened after Afghanistan?"

"I was at Walter Reed for six months. Honorably discharged. I used the GI Bill to go to school to become a nurse."

"Were you interested in medicine before you were injured?" Debbie asked.

"Absolutely not. I had no idea what I was interested in. But the nurses and the doctors took such good care of me that I wanted to learn how to do that for others. After I got my bachelor's, I went on and became a nurse practitioner. I work in Colorado Springs in a family medicine clinic, and my wife is a critical care nurse at the local hospital. We've been married ten years. I healed physically and made progress emotionally, and she's been a huge part of that."

"Kids?" Debbie asked.

"One girl." Thom smiled, and his eyes lit up. "Madeline Reed. It turns out Reed can be a girl's name too, although it's more commonly used for boys. I hope you don't mind us using it."

"Not at all." Tears stung Debbie's eyes. "I can't think of a better way to honor him."

"I'm so glad you think so." His eyes glistened. "I wish I'd told you ten years ago when she was born. I shouldn't have waited so long."

"I understand," Debbie said. "Do you have a picture of her?"

He took out his phone and flipped it around to show a photo of a girl with a head full of curly dark hair and her father's kind smile. "She didn't get her hair from me," Thom joked. Then he swiped the screen. The next photo was of Madeline, Thom, and a woman with thick dark hair and brown eyes.

"She's darling," Debbie said. "And your wife is gorgeous. What's her name?"

"Elena."

"You have a beautiful family."

"I do. And I'm missing them terribly. I've never been away from them before. But I need to help my grandmother. It's the right thing to do."

"That's really good of you," Debbie told him.

He put his phone on the table. "I have the family you should have had."

"No," Debbie replied firmly. "You have the family you were meant to have."

"Don't get me wrong," Thom said. "I know all about survivor's guilt. I've worked through that, as well as everything else, including PTSD. But the bottom line is that I have what I have because of Captain Brandt. I'm living a better life than I ever could have dreamed, and I wouldn't have seen any of it if not for his sacrifice."

"Because he did the right thing," Debbie said. "He wouldn't have had it any other way. He was your commanding officer. Once you were injured, he had to get you out of there. He did what was required of him. He knew that. I knew that, from the bare-bones story I was told. And his parents knew that too."

"I think of Reed every day," Thom said. "I'll be eternally grateful."

"Someday in eternity, you'll be able to tell him," Debbie said. "If he doesn't know already."

"I've thought that too." He glanced at her left hand. "What about you? Did you find someone else and get married after all?"

She shook her head. "The timing hasn't been right, and my life has been full. But if God has plans for a marriage for me, it will happen." She hesitated, then added, "I am dating someone though, for the first time since Reed."

"I'll remember you in my prayers."

"Thank you." Debbie exhaled slowly. "You know that Reed did what was required of him. But you did what was required of you too. You were injured and had PTSD, but you didn't leave it at that. You got help and did the work to heal. You chose a profession where you help other people and pay forward the care that was given to you. You have a good marriage. You're raising a little girl. You've definitely done what was required of you, and then some."

Thom's lower lip trembled, and he took a moment to collect himself. "When I found out Captain Brandt had been killed, I vowed to myself that I wouldn't waste what he sacrificed for me. I hope I never will."

"You won't," Debbie said. "I can tell that from what you've said to me. Thank you. I'm glad you worked up the courage it must have taken to track me down."

Thom met her gaze and then cleared his throat. "Actually, there's one more reason I came. Do you have a few more minutes?"

"Yes. Let me get us more coffee." It seemed there was something else he needed to say. Maybe another cup of coffee and a strawberry scone would help him say it.

When she got back to the table, there was a small medallion in the middle of it.

Debbie put down the plate of scones and then emptied the coffeepot into Thom's mug. "What is that?" But as soon as the last word came out of her mouth, she knew. She returned the empty pot to its machine then sat at the table once more.

"Reed gave it to me when he shoved me into the truck," Thom said. "He didn't say anything about it, but he didn't have to. He'd showed it to me when we arrived in Afghanistan and said that you'd given it to him."

"I did," Debbie murmured.

He touched the medallion. "I put it in my jacket pocket, which they had to cut off me. They stored it with my other personal items. Once I was released from Walter Reed, I put it in my footlocker.

A few years later, I moved to Colorado, all the while intending to track you down. Then last month I was invited to speak at the local VFW right before I came to help my grandmother. I went through my footlocker for a pair of dress shoes to wear with my uniform, and I came across this." He picked up the medallion and handed it to Debbie. "I'm mortified it took me so long to get it back to you."

Debbie picked up the medallion, staring at the image of the young woman in the center. "I bought this for Reed at a yard sale. We'd watched a movie about Joan of Arc soon after we started dating, and he was intrigued by her. It impressed me that he was inspired by her, a girl from six centuries ago. I'd always found Joan of Arc fascinating, and she became an inspirational figure for both of us." She held up the medallion. "I didn't realize he'd taken this with him."

"He carried it with him wherever he went. He'd want you to have it."

"Thank you so much." Debbie wrapped her hand around the medallion. Not once had she wondered what happened to it when Reed had died, but she was happy to have it now.

Debbie walked Thom to the depot lobby and gave him a hug. Then she returned to the café and sat back down at the table to finish her cold coffee.

"Wow, Lord," she said out loud as she set the medallion on the table. "Just wow."

Telling his story had no doubt been good for Thom. But it had also been good for her. Reed's sacrifice hadn't gone to waste. And

Thom's was only one story. There were other men who had been saved because of Reed. And yet he'd been thinking of her in the midst of the battle, as he faced capture. He'd given the medallion to Thom for her.

Debbie took her phone from her pocket and sent Betsy a text about her meeting with Thom. Then she added, HE NAMED HIS DAUGHTER MADELINE REED. SHE'S TEN.

Betsy replied, I'M TOUCHED. IT MEANS THE WORLD TO ME THAT THOM GAVE HER REED'S NAME.

Debbie sent another text about the Joan of Arc medallion, ending with, I'M NOT SURE WHAT I'LL DO WITH IT.

YOU'LL KNOW WHAT TO DO WITH IT WHEN THE TIME COMES, Betsy texted back.

YOU'RE RIGHT, I WILL. AND I HAVE SOMETHING TO SHARE WITH YOU I THINK YOU'LL WANT TO HEAR. Reed had asked Thom not to share the details of his death with his parents, but Debbie was sure that Betsy would want to know how Reed had sacrificed his life for his men.

Betsy responded with a heart emoji. Debbie stood and tucked the medallion into her apron pocket. She took her mug to the kitchen to clean up and get ready for the next day.

Listening to Thom's story made Debbie think of Ray. When he talked about his war experiences, he left out the gruesome details. She'd thought that was because he wanted to spare the listeners' feelings, but maybe in the eighty years that had passed his memory had faded. Perhaps in another fifty years, Thom wouldn't remember the troubling details.

Perhaps she wouldn't either.

After she finished her work, she retrieved the medallion from her apron pocket and put it in her purse. Then she checked her phone to see if she'd heard back from the tourist society on Guernsey. Nothing.

She had waited long enough. She found the Guernsey Police Headquarters site. There was a button to request public information, which seemed like a legitimate option. All she needed was information on Oliver Godfrey that would be public. When had he lived on Guernsey? Was he who he said he was?

Before she could talk herself out of it, she clicked the button and filled out the form.

It was three thirty. Too early for dinner. And she was too restless to go home. What she really wanted to do was check in with Ray. So she called him.

He answered on the third ring. "Hello, Debbie. How are you?"

"Good. Except I haven't made any progress on finding your jacket."

"Oh, that's all right. How did your meeting with Reed's soldier friend go?"

"Really well."

"Want to come and tell me about it?"

Debbie sighed with relief. "Yes, I would. I've been thinking about your story."

"So have I," he said. "Come on over."

CHAPTER THIRTEEN

When Ray reached Alié and Anne's great-uncle, the man seemed confused.

"Bonsoir, Monsieur," *Ray said.* "Je suis *Ray Zink.*"

"Ah," *the uncle answered.* "Le musicien américain."

"Oui." *Ray tried to remember the little bit of French he'd picked up. Thankfully, Clark and Edith caught up with him.* "Remember Alié and Anne's great-uncle, Sarge?"

"Certainly." *Sergeant Clark shook the older man's hand.*

Ray turned to Edith. "How's your French?"

"Passable. What would you like me to ask him?"

"Why he's here. How the rest of his family is."

Edith introduced herself and then began asking questions. The elderly man answered in rapid
French. Ray could only catch a few words—oui, Anne
est malade, est allée à Paris. Ray concentrated on what
they were saying. Who went to Paris? Anne? Because
she was ill?

Edith said, "Merci," and then faced Ray and
Sergeant Clark. "Monsieur Beaufoy—"

Ray realized they'd never been told his last name.
Naturally, it wasn't Dumas.

Edith continued. "He said that after most of
the Americans left, his grandniece Anne's illness became
worse. The older niece—"

"Alié," Clark supplied.

"Yes." Edith seemed a little confused. "She left for
Paris soon after it was liberated. Then their mother
became ill. He couldn't find a doctor to examine the
mother, so he hired someone to get her to the train
station and on to Paris. But the younger girl stayed
with him—until he grew concerned that her heart was
failing her."

Ray sucked in a breath.

"An American Red Cross worker in the area got
them on a ferry to England and then brought them to
the hospital yesterday. He said the crossing was bitter

cold, which couldn't have done Anne any good. He has no idea if the doctors here can help her. He tried to contact the girl's mother in Paris through the Red Cross a few days ago but hasn't heard back from her yet."

"Could we go see Anne?" Ray asked. "Is she strong enough for a visit?"

Edith spoke to Monsieur Beaufoy, who shrugged.

"I'll go in and see if it's all right." Edith slipped into the building.

Monsieur Beaufoy continued to smoke his cigarette. He didn't exactly smile at Ray, but he didn't frown either.

Edith poked her head out the door. "Anne would love to see both of you." She motioned for them to follow her.

Monsieur Beaufoy put out his cigarette. Clark followed Edith while Ray motioned for Monsieur Beaufoy to go next. Then he brought up the rear.

Anne sat up on a cot in a long row of women and children. "Ray." She beamed and then spoke in French.

"She wants to know what you're doing here," Edith translated.

Ray smiled. "Bonsoir, Anne." Then he said to Edith, "Tell her Sergeant Clark and I were both *wounded in the Netherlands and recovered here, but we're fine now."*

The conversation continued as Edith translated, about Alié, their mother, and how Anne liked being in the army hospital.

In English she said, "There's food." She wrinkled her nose. "It is not so good. But I am thankful for it." Everyone laughed.

"Would it be all right if we come back tomorrow?" Ray asked.

Edith translated, and Anne beamed and said, "Bien sûr." *Ray knew that meant* of course.

After they said goodbye to Anne and Monsieur Beaufoy and stepped out into the rain, Ray asked Edith, "Did you have a chance to read Anne's chart? Or speak with her nurse before you brought us in?"

She shook her head. "I'll try to speak with her nurse tomorrow."

When they returned Christmas afternoon, Alié was at Anne's side on the cot and Monsieur Beaufoy sat in a straight-backed chair beside it.

Alié smiled when she saw Ray. "I was afraid Anne and Grand-Oncle had imagined you. But you're really here."

"Yes." Ray reached out to give her a hug, but she reached him first and kissed both his cheeks. "How are you holding up?" he asked.

"All right. Paris isn't any better than Normandy—at least we had food there—but we're getting by. Maman is resting and trying to regain her health. I came to see if I should take Anne to Paris, but I think she'll get better care here. The doctors and nurses seem to be very good."

"What is the diagnosis?" Ray asked.

"Rheumatic heart disease. Her heart valves are damaged."

"What is the treatment?" Ray asked.

"Rest. Good nutrition," Alié answered.

"There's been some use of cortisone as treatment also," Edith added. "With some success. Did the doctor mention that?"

"No." Alié glanced at Anne.

"I'll talk to the nurse about it." Edith started toward a nurse at the end of the row of cots.

Sergeant Clark stepped closer to Alié. "How is Paris?"

"Intact. By some miracle." Alié abruptly turned to Ray. "Have you found a piano to play around here?"

He smiled. "There's one in the mess hall."

"Do you think we could go there?"

"I want to go," Anne said in English.

Alié spoke rapidly to her in French.

Anne frowned and crossed her arms.

Alié teased in English, "You're feeling better, I see." Then she nodded to where Edith spoke with Anne's nurse. "Who is your friend?"

When Sergeant Clark didn't say anything, Ray said, "Edith cared for both of us when we were patients here. And she and Sergeant Clark have become friends."

Sergeant Clark cleared his throat as Alié stepped closer to Ray. "I'm happy to hear she's his friend, not yours."

Ray's face grew warm. Was Alié flirting with him? That was the last thing he wanted. His heart was spoken for.

As Edith joined them once more, Alié said, "We could go sing Christmas carols."

"That's a great idea." Sergeant Clark nudged Ray.

Anne said something in French, and Edith answered, "I'll speak with your nurse and find a wheelchair."

A couple of minutes later Edith returned with a wheelchair. Alié grabbed the blanket off the bed, and when Anne was settled in the chair, Alié tucked it around her. Ray pushed Anne out of the building and along the gravel path. When they reached the mess hall, Sergeant Clark and Ray lifted the chair and walked up the steps. A few doctors and nurses were sitting at the tables in the back of the room and drinking tea.

Edith stayed close to Sergeant Clark as the group gathered around the piano. Ray pulled out the piano bench, recalling how he'd played in this room during the noon meal and at two dances. It was good to be in Wraxall again.

He gave Anne a smile and began playing "Silent Night."

Alié, Sergeant Clark, and Edith sang along in English while Anne sang in French. Monsieur Beaufoy joined Anne. Ray had never heard anything so heavenly in his life—except for Eleanor's singing.

For a moment he felt overcome with homesickness. For his family and for Eleanor. And yet he had so much to be thankful for. He was under a roof in a dry mess hall, not hunkered down in a wet, cold, muddy foxhole. He was safe. He was with people he cared about. He had meaningful work ahead of him.

Meaningful but dangerous work.

He continued playing carol after carol. "Joy to the World." "O Little Town of Bethlehem." "We Three Kings."

As he played, he glanced at the others, sure heaven was close on this Christmas evening—to this group and to his loved ones back home.

But they were still on earth. During a war that had shattered the world as they knew it. Who knew what tomorrow would bring for any of them?

The next morning Sergeant Clark went to the burn ward to tell Edith goodbye and then went with Ray to tell Anne, Alié, and Monsieur Beaufoy farewell too. Sergeant Clark took Alié's hand and said, "I'd like to speak with you in private."

"Non," she said in a teasing voice. "You have a girlfriend."

Sergeant Clark shook his head. "I have eyes only for you."

Alié laughed and hooked her arm through Ray's. "I'd much rather speak in private to Specialist Zink."

Sergeant Clark took a step backward, a surprised expression on his face.

"She's teasing," Ray said.

"Actually, I'm not." Alié squeezed his arm.

"Well." Sergeant Clark's voice faltered a little. "Zink has a sweetheart back home." Then he said, "We'd better be on our way."

"Where are you going?" Alié asked.

"It could be anywhere that bomb disposal units are needed. Maybe even Paris." Now he was teasing.

"Oh, I hope so," Alié said.

Ray couldn't understand why Sergeant Clark was teasing her. They were headed back to Cornwall. And why would Paris be a possibility? The city hadn't been mined like so many other locations across Europe.

Sergeant Clark and Ray arrived in Cornwall in the early afternoon. Ray checked his mail and was surprised to find a box among the letters from his parents and sister.

He opened the box. It was his Purple Heart.

Clark peered over his shoulder. "Good. Maybe that means mine will be here soon."

Ray didn't reply. Who knew how things came about in the army? He was shocked that his had come so soon. Lieutenant Hollingsworth must have put the paperwork in the day Ray was wounded. But surely he'd put in Sergeant Clark's too.

The months ticked by. January, February, March, and April.

On May 2, news came that Hitler was dead. The first report was that he had died fighting, but few believed that. What everyone did believe was that the war would soon be over.

On May 4, Ray returned to the hospital in Wraxall while Sergeant Clark was detained in Cornwall. He said he'd try to get away if possible. Ray guessed Anne would be gone, but he wanted to check for sure. He went into the ward she'd been in before but couldn't find her. He asked a nurse about Edith at the entrance to the burn ward.

"I'll get her," the nurse said.

A few minutes later, Edith came out. "Ray! Did you know Leland is here?"

"What? How did he get here so fast?"

"He caught a ride with an officer coming this way. He's probably in the barracks by now. He said he has a new assignment."

"Does he know where he's going yet?"

She shook her head. "He hopes to find out today."

Ray hadn't gotten his next assignment yet. He hoped it was with Sergeant Clark.

Edith asked, "What can I help you with?"

"I was wondering if you knew anything about Anne Dumas, the French girl we visited at Christmas."

"I do," Edith said. "She's been staying with me. Alié is coming to get her tomorrow to take her to Paris."

That news made Ray happy. It would be good to see the Dumas sisters. "How is Anne doing?"

"As well as can be expected," Edith answered. "She'll never get her strength back entirely, but she's strong enough to travel. The cortisone shots have helped."

Anne was a brave girl. "That's good of you to help the family out."

"I adore both Anne and Alié," Edith said. "I get off in a few minutes. Leland is going to meet me at my place. You can come along and see him and Anne at the same time."

Fifteen minutes later, Edith opened the door to the house where she was boarding. Sergeant Clark stood in the living room while Anne made her way down the stairs.

"Ray!" Anne called out.

Sergeant Clark stood. "Specialist Zink. I've seen our next set of orders. We're going to the island of Guernsey to clear mines as soon as this all ends. It should be any day now." He clapped Ray on the back. "We'll continue to serve side by side, hopefully until we return home."

CHAPTER FOURTEEN

The next morning Debbie checked her email on her phone before she got out of bed. She had a reply from the society site on the island of Guernsey.

> *I do not know nor have I heard of a Mr. Oliver Godfrey from Guernsey. I was, however, acquainted with Adele Martin Harris. She passed away thirteen years ago. I remember her two daughters but don't remember a son. I'm terribly sorry I can't be of more help.*
> *Sincerely,*
> *April Edwards*
> *The Isle of Guernsey Society Secretary, Bailiwick of Guernsey*

Debbie emailed April back, thanking her for her reply and adding, *If you come across any information about Oliver Godfrey, please let me know.*

She didn't have a reply from the Guernsey police about Oliver. Was he really who he said he was? Why would he come so far to meet Ray and then disappear, perhaps taking the jacket with him? All of it was puzzling.

When Debbie arrived at the café, Janet was taking fresh scones from the oven. After the baking was done and before the first customers arrived, the two had a chance to chat.

"I got a couple of texts from my friend Cassie, who worked with Jonathon Bell," Janet said as she organized omelet toppings. "She described an odd interaction with him yesterday."

"Really? What happened?"

"She had a consulting session with him, and he took a phone call in the middle of their meeting. She only heard his side of the conversation, but he said, 'Yeah, I have it. You can see from the picture I posted it's in perfect shape. It's been in a velvet box for the last eighty years. You want it now? All right, give me half an hour.' Then he told Cassie that an interview he'd been chasing had come available and he needed to reschedule their meeting."

Debbie shoved her hand in the pocket of her strawberry apron. "How strange."

"Jonathon didn't have any stories on the news that evening."

"Maybe it will air on tonight's news."

"She said there's nothing on the schedule."

"Interesting." Debbie sighed. "Well, those stories take a while to put together, right? Perhaps it's a feature story and not a news story. Jonathon does a lot of feature stories, like with Ray."

"Yes, but they're still timely." Janet stepped to the sink and washed her hands. "Both stories on Ray ran the days he did the interviews."

"That's true," Debbie answered. "I'll do some searching online to see if I can find out where he posts items to sell." Jonathon wouldn't have fit through the window, but he could have convinced or even hired someone else to climb through for him.

"I told Cassie that Representative Clark was in town the evening the jacket was stolen too, along with her niece Ruby." Janet tied her apron tighter. "Cassie and her husband are friends with Ruby's dad. According to Cassie, the siblings are very different. Heather Clark is driven and single-minded. Her brother is a teacher and much more laid-back."

"Interesting," Debbie said.

"Ruby is the sole grandchild in the family, and it seems Heather, according to Cassie, has been making a concerted effort to influence her to carry on the family legacy," Janet said. "It's caused a bit of a rift between Heather and her brother."

"I wonder if that's why Heather wanted Ruby to have Leland Clark's Purple Heart, as a part of his legacy."

"Maybe," Janet said. "Anyway, I'll look more into Ruby and see if she would have been motivated to take Ray's jacket."

The café grew busy. Patricia, Harry, and Crosby came in, along with other regulars. Then a group of tourists came in for breakfast before the museum opened. Debbie barely kept up with the bustling tables until Paulette arrived. Janet left at noon to spend time with Tiffany, and Debbie took over the kitchen. Again, she and Paulette had to hustle to get all the orders out and keep up with clearing the tables.

At two, Debbie flipped the sign to Closed with a flourish. "Made it." She laughed. Some days she felt as if she were attempting to sprint a marathon.

"I can stay and help clean up," Paulette said.

"That's okay," Debbie said. "I can do it."

Paulette untied her strawberry apron. "Greg told me you've been looking into his grandfather's World War II service."

"I have," Debbie answered.

"Thank you for doing that," Paulette said. "Greg's grandmother, Vivian, didn't talk about her first husband much. She remarried after the war, a good man who was kind to her kids, including EJ." That was the name Earl Jr., Paulette's husband and Greg's father, often went by. "They had three more children for a total of seven, so they were all busy. I don't think she intentionally deprived EJ of information about his dad, but not knowing created a big hole in his life. It would be great if Greg and the boys got more of the story."

"I think so too." Debbie considered what Thom had told her about Reed's capture and how much it meant to her to know those details.

"Are you all right?" Paulette asked.

Debbie realized that she had been silent for several moments. She smiled. "I'm fine." She reached for Paulette's apron. "I'll put this in the laundry."

"Thank you." Paulette headed toward the kitchen. "I'll just grab my purse."

As Debbie cleaned, she thought about what she needed to do when she got home. Research Oliver Godfrey's background and Jonathon Bell's World War II memorabilia business. Oh, and one more thing.

She needed to find out when Leland Clark first started claiming that he'd saved a girl's life on Guernsey.

When Debbie arrived home she poured herself a glass of lemonade, grabbed her laptop, and headed out to the table on the back porch. She decided to start with Leland Clark's claim that he was the one who'd saved Adele Martin.

It took longer than she thought it would. She couldn't find it in any of his biographical information. She clicked on the *Columbus Dispatch* archives and searched for *Leland Clark*. There were hundreds of results. She sighed as she scanned them. None of the titles included anything about him saving a girl on Guernsey after World War II ended.

She decided to go back to the first result, from March 1962. It was a short article about Leland Clark, who worked as a prosecutor for the city of Columbus, announcing he was running for the Ohio House of Representatives. The next article was also short. Leland had spoken at a meeting of the Columbus Chamber of Commerce. The article mentioned that he was a World War II vet who had served in Europe. He'd graduated from Vanderbilt University Law School in Nashville. He hadn't gone to Harvard, but he had gone to a good school nonetheless.

She continued to skim articles. He had won in November and then run for reelection two years later. In 1966, he had run—and won—again.

In the spring of 1968, Leland ran for the Ohio Senate. Debbie clicked on an article about a debate he participated in that was hosted by the Columbus Club. She skimmed the article, and the word *Guernsey* caught her eye.

> *Representative Clark spoke of his service during World War II, including clearing land mines on the island of Guernsey after the war ended. In June of 1945, Clark saved the life of a local girl who ran across a minefield.*

There it was. In 1968 he had publicly made the claim that he'd saved the life of a girl on Guernsey. Debbie couldn't know for sure that it was the first time, but presumably he'd repeated the story for decades. Who knew how often he told it at home? No doubt for most of Heather's life.

She kept scrolling. He told the same story the following month during an interview then repeated it four years later when he ran for the Ohio Senate position again, which he won. He continued to serve in the Ohio General Assembly until he was eighty-one and had reached his term limit.

He died nine years later in 2013. Debbie found his obituary. His wife, Isabella Adams Clark, had died in 2006. They'd been married fifty-four years. He was survived by his two children, Heather Anne Clark and James Leland Clark, and one grandchild, Ruby Clark.

She went back and bookmarked several pages then focused her search on Jonathon Bell. She opened several different resale sights. No one by the name of Jonathon Bell was selling World War II memorabilia. Though that didn't necessarily prove anything. He might be selling under an assumed name.

Next she began going through World War II memorabilia sites. There were so many. She found jackets, hats, helmets, boots, mess kits, and medals. She couldn't find any jackets that matched Ray's. She couldn't be sure about the medals though.

As she scrolled through the sites, one named Ring the World War II Bell caught her eye. She found a couple of jackets—again, none of them matched Ray's—several helmets, bayonets, and medals. People could leave questions or comments below the items. There was a comment below a Purple Heart for sale dated a month before that read, *Administrator: Purchased from an estate sale near Cleveland, Ohio.*

Underneath that was another comment dated two weeks before. *Jonathon, I'm interested in this. I'll give you a call. HAC*

Did HAC stand for Heather Anne Clark?

Debbie took out her phone, trying to decide if she should call Jonathon or Heather first. Instead of doing either, she decided to take a brisk walk to clear her head. It wouldn't do any good to fly off the handle at either of them.

Twenty minutes later, Debbie arrived back at her house and decided to call Heather. She grabbed her laptop and headed to the porch again then pulled out her phone. It was four thirty. Hopefully, Heather was available.

"Representative Clark's phone. This is Ruby. How can I help you?"

Debbie said, "Hi, Ruby. It's Debbie Albright from Dennison. Is your aunt available?"

"Oh, hi." Ruby's voice was soft but cheerful. "No, Heather's not here. She's out on a run. Can I have her call you back?"

"Please." Debbie rattled off her phone number. "I have a few questions for her."

"I'll let her know," Ruby said. "Anything I can help you with in the meantime?"

"I'm still trying to figure out what happened to Ray's jacket."

"What do you mean?"

"It's missing. Our police chief called Heather about it."

"Oh. She didn't say anything to me." Ruby cleared her throat. "Or maybe she did, but I forgot." That seemed unlikely to Debbie.

"Do you mind if I ask you a couple of questions?" Debbie asked.

Ruby cleared her throat again. "If you have questions, you should talk to Heather, not me." Before Debbie could respond, Ruby blurted, "Nice chatting with you. Bye!" She hung up.

Debbie held her phone in her hand for a long minute. She wouldn't say for sure that Ruby was acting suspiciously, but she wasn't exactly acting normal either. She put her phone on the table and picked up her pen to write some notes.

Heather was off on a run. She had to be in her sixties. Debbie admired her energy and dedication. She wouldn't be running when she was Heather's age, but she certainly planned to be as active as possible. For a moment she wondered if Heather could have climbed into the window. Maybe that was what Ruby was hiding. No, that didn't seem plausible. But Debbie couldn't rule it out entirely.

Should she call Jonathon?

She picked up her phone just as it started to buzz with an incoming call from Heather.

She pushed the accept button. "Hi, Heather. Thank you for getting back to me."

"Of course," she said, a little out of breath. "I hope you have good news. Has Ray's jacket turned up?"

"I'm afraid not," Debbie answered.

"That's too bad. What can I help you with?"

"I searched online for the jacket to see if someone's trying to sell it. I didn't find the jacket, but I did find a site called Ring the World War II Bell. It looks as if the administrator has ties to Ohio. Someone with the initials HAC referred to the administrator as Jonathon in the comments."

Heather laughed, apparently anticipating what Debbie was about to ask. "You're quite the sleuth."

"Would that happen to be a conversation between you and Jonathon Bell?"

"Well, I wouldn't want to admit to the public that I was interested in buying a Purple Heart, but I'll admit it to you. Yes, that was Jonathon and me," Heather said. "But I want you to know that I didn't buy the Purple Heart. As much as I want one in my dad's memory, I couldn't bring myself to buy someone else's. I called Jonathon to let him know that, which is when he told me he was interviewing a man in Dennison named Ray Zink. And then, like I said earlier, he sent me a picture, and I recognized that Ray was the man in the photo that was on Dad's desk. By the way, Jonathon thinks Ray stole Dad's story about rescuing the girl on Guernsey too."

"Really? I thought he was trying to be impartial."

"No. He knew Dad. He knew he wouldn't lie," Heather said. "Any other questions?"

Debbie hesitated, then decided it wouldn't do any good trying to change Heather's mind about the story. "Yes," she said. "Would you tell me about your mother?"

"What does she have to do with any of this?"

"Nothing," Debbie said. "I'm just curious."

"They met when Dad was overseas," Heather answered. "Her name was Isabella Adams Clark."

"Where was she from?"

"England. Dad met her before he was transferred to Guernsey. They kept in touch through the years, and she came to the US in 1951. They married eight months later."

Debbie wondered when Leland Clark had broken things off with Edith.

But before Debbie could ask another question, Heather said, "I need to get back to work, but I want to state again that I'm positive Ray stole Dad's story. Somehow Oliver Godfrey got the two American soldiers confused."

"I'm equally positive that Ray rescued Adele Martin," Debbie said firmly. She needed to prove it somehow, most likely through documents from Guernsey or the US Army or the Royal Engineers.

"Well, at this point there's no way to really know, is there? All we have are the fuzzy memories of an old man."

Debbie inhaled sharply then counted to ten to make sure she could respond in an even tone. "I'll do some research and let you know what I find."

"Please do," Heather said. "And let me know when you find Ray's jacket too, would you?"

"Yes. Yes, I will." Regardless of her rising blood pressure, Debbie managed to say, "Goodbye, Heather."

After she hung up, she stared at the phone for a long time. She would prove that Ray was the honest one, no matter what it took.

CHAPTER FIFTEEN

nstead of calling Jonathon next, Debbie continued her research, tracking down the website of the police department on Guernsey and finding the nonemergency phone number.

The call went to a voice mail menu. Debbie listened closely to the different departments. Criminal Investigation, Guernsey Border Agent, High-Tech Crime Unit, Neighborhood Policing Team, Police Bomb Disposal Unit.

Debbie found that interesting. Perhaps there were still mines found from time to time, even now.

She kept listening. Public Protection Unit, Special Constables.

She selected the Neighborhood Policing Team, which sounded like her best option.

She left a message. "Hello. My name is Debbie Albright, and I live in the United States, in Dennison, Ohio. I'm looking for information on an Oliver Godfrey, who claims to have grown up on Guernsey. This is in regards to a World War II veteran who helped clear mines there at the end of the war. The veteran saved a little girl's life. Her name was Adele Martin, and she was Oliver Godfrey's mother. We're five hours behind you, so please call after noon your time. Thank you."

She ended the call and hunted for more information on the bomb disposal unit. Their website included information about the German occupation during the war. After the liberation, German engineers cleared the minefields, supervised by Royal Engineers. That was the group Ray had worked with.

After the minefield clearing was completed, the Guernsey Police were trained to deal with any additional mines that were found. Officers had dealt with thousands of them over the years.

It was hard to imagine having that sort of threat in one's homeland, but Debbie knew it was the case for many people around the world. All wars left long-lasting dangers to civilian populations.

Debbie closed the website and checked her email. She had another letter from the secretary of the Isle of Guernsey Society, April Edwards.

> *Miss Albright, I asked one of our members about Oliver Godfrey. It turns out Adele Martin Harris's first husband had the last name of Godfrey, so I stand corrected. It seems Oliver Godfrey could be her son after all. Perhaps an older child who left the island before I arrived. My regrets for the mistake.*

Debbie quickly wrote April back, asking for the name and email address of the woman who had remembered Adele Martin's previous marriage. Maybe she had more information about Adele, or knew of someone who might. Maybe she could even put Debbie in touch with his half siblings, who might know how to contact him.

Debbie's phone dinged with a text from her mom.

DAD AND I ARE GOING OUT TO BUONA VITA TONIGHT. WANT TO GO WITH US? WE CAN MEET YOU THERE AT 6:30.

Buona Vita Italian Restaurant's food was delicious. She texted back, YES PLEASE! SEE YOU SOON.

She closed her laptop, realizing how unsettled she felt about her conversation with Heather and the woman's accusations about Ray. Just the thought of spending time with her parents made her feel better. She'd tell them about her phone call with Heather and get their feedback on it. She always appreciated her parents' advice.

Debbie sat down at the last booth, placed her hands on the marble-topped table, and leaned against the back of the booth. It was the same one Mom, Dad, and she had sat in the night she had been inducted into the National Honor Society. They sat in it the night before the first day of her senior year of high school. The night before they had driven her to Cleveland for college. It was the same booth they'd sat in when Reed came to Dennison with her to ask for her parents' blessing to marry her. And it was the same booth they'd sat in when she told them she was buying the Whistle Stop Café with Janet and moving home.

Debbie smiled at her thoughts as she spotted her parents coming toward her. Both broke into big smiles when they saw Debbie.

After they'd ordered—caprese salad for an appetizer and shrimp alfredo for all three of them—Mom leaned across the table. "How was your meeting with Reed's fellow soldier?"

"Oops. I forgot to text you about that," Debbie said.

"It's okay. Something tells me it's better told in person."

"That's true." Debbie explained how well it had gone and what he'd told her about the attack in Afghanistan. "Thom named his daughter Madeline Reed."

"How wonderful," her mom said. "Thom really respected Reed, didn't he?"

Debbie nodded. "And Thom returned a Joan of Arc medallion that I'd given Reed not too long after we first started dating. Reed had asked him to do that if anything happened to him, and he gave it to Thom right before he surrendered." She took out her phone and pulled up a photo to show her parents. "I took a picture of it last night when I put it in my jewelry box. Reed was impressed with Joan of Arc's faith, courage, and leadership."

"All qualities that Reed himself possessed," Mom said. "Do you plan to keep in touch with Thom?"

Debbie leaned back in the booth. "We didn't talk about that, but I wouldn't mind staying in touch. It wasn't as hard as I thought it would be to hear what he had to say. But there's something else that's bothering me right now. It has to do with Ray." She told them about the conversation with Heather.

Dad bristled. "You're not serious. She's accusing Ray of lying?"

"Yes. And of stealing her dad's story." Debbie told them about the articles from the Columbus newspaper where Leland Clark had claimed he'd saved the life of a girl on Guernsey. "So it's not like Heather doesn't have a reason to think her father was the one who saved the girl. That's probably what she's been told her whole life."

"Obviously, he told that story to get elected," Mom said.

"It would seem out of character for him to do that though," Debbie said. "He served valiantly during the war. He was injured and returned to service. He graduated law school and had a career in law and politics. The first record I could find of him telling the story was when he was running to be a representative."

"Which makes sense," Dad said. "Maybe he saw it as 'borrowing' Ray's story."

"And that was long before the internet," Mom said. "He could be fairly certain that Ray would never know. If Ray happened to read about it in the newspaper, Leland probably counted on Ray not calling him out."

Debbie took a drink of water. "Ray wrote Leland at his office when he read about him being elected as a state senator. Once when he was in Columbus, he even called Leland's office and left a message. But Leland never got back to him."

"And no wonder," Dad said. "He'd already appropriated Ray's story. If he met with Ray, it would have been more likely for the truth to come out."

"What do you mean?"

"Well, let's say they met at a restaurant, and a friend of Leland's approached them. Leland would be obliged to introduce Ray. Even if he didn't mention that they served together in World War II, Ray might add that Clark was his sergeant. Then the friend of Clark's might ask Ray if he was with Clark when he rescued the girl on Guernsey."

"Awkward," Debbie said.

"Exactly." Dad crossed his arms. "It makes perfect sense that Leland never answered Ray's letter or returned his call. It would threaten not only his fabrication but his career."

Mom drummed her fingers on the table. "He probably didn't think of that when he first told the story."

Dad agreed. "Probably not. In fact, I imagine he told the story impulsively, feeling he needed a boost during the debate. Stealing the story probably came from his own insecurities."

Debbie remembered Ray mentioning that Leland Clark nearly broke down during intense fighting. Perhaps he felt embarrassed about that afterward, and claiming that he'd rescued the girl made him feel better about himself. Ray was sympathetic to Leland's struggles, saying all soldiers had a breaking point. Perhaps the political debate was another near breaking point for Leland Clark.

The waiter delivered their food, and the conversation shifted to Oliver Godfrey's disappearance. "Did he say anything to you last week about where else he planned to travel?" Debbie asked. "I saw the three of you chatting."

"Oliver told us there was someone in Minnesota he hoped to see," Mom said. "He didn't have a phone number, but he'd sent an email a couple of weeks before. He was still hoping to hear back from them. Maybe he did."

"Interesting," Debbie said. Perhaps he hadn't simply disappeared. Perhaps he had an innocent reason for leaving so early the next day.

Halfway through dinner, Dad said, "You have a lot of interactions going on right now, all war-related. How are you doing?"

"Really well, actually," Debbie said. "I have a research project that I'm working on too, checking out information about Greg's grandfather. Kim told me how to request information from the National Archives, and I passed it on to Greg. If Ray doesn't have his army records, I'll see what I can find for him at the same time I'm doing research on Greg's grandfather. If we're lucky, there's a record of Ray rescuing the girl on Guernsey." She'd take no joy in exposing Leland Clark's deception, but she couldn't let Ray be made out to be a liar.

The next morning after the breakfast rush, Debbie texted Thom. I SO ENJOYED OUR VISIT YESTERDAY. IF YOU THINK OF ANYTHING ELSE YOU'D LIKE TO SHARE, PLEASE FEEL FREE TO REACH OUT. AND IF YOUR FAMILY EVER COMES TO OHIO, I'D LOVE TO MEET THEM.

Debbie had just flipped the sign to Closed and started cleanup when her phone rang. It wasn't a number in her contacts. In fact, it had a +44 code.

She answered it. "Hello?"

"This is Officer Rick Jones with the Guernsey Police." He spoke with a strong British accent. "I'm returning your call."

"Thank you. It's good to hear from you." Debbie briefly relayed the story of Oliver coming to Ohio and meeting an American World War II vet who had helped to clear minefields on Guernsey. "The next morning, the veteran's World War II jacket disappeared and Oliver Godfrey had unexpectedly left town. I was wondering if you have any record of him. Is he a reliable person? Should we be worried about him leaving so unexpectedly?"

"Interesting," Officer Jones replied.

Debbie laughed. "I'm afraid it all sounds a little outlandish. I've heard that he may have wanted to visit someone in Minnesota. I've also been in touch with the Isle of Guernsey Society and learned that he might still have half siblings on the island. But there's only so much I can do from here."

"Well, I'll admit this is a first for me, but it sounds as if your intentions are good." Debbie could hear the smile in the officer's voice. "I'll ask around and see what I can find."

"Thank you. I appreciate any information you can give me."

After Debbie finished closing the café, she headed for Good Shepherd. It was four o'clock. If Ray had taken a nap, he'd most likely be awake by now. She'd have time to chat with him before his dinner was served.

She wanted to take something to him, something to brighten his day. She hurried home and cut several roses and forget-me-nots. She arranged them in a bouquet and placed them in a canning jar with a bow of twine tied around it.

When she arrived at Good Shepherd, Ray was in the courtyard, reading what appeared to be a very old book.

Debbie approached him with the flowers. "Good afternoon, Ray. What are you reading?"

He held it up so she could see the cover, with his thumb holding his place. "*The War Poems of Siegfried Sassoon*. I've had it since high school." It *was* an old book. "The author served in World War I." He squinted a little and shaded his eyes with his free hand. "How are you?"

"Good, although your jacket still hasn't been found."

"That's all right." He sighed. "I talked with Trudy on the phone this morning. As you suggested, I asked if she wanted my jacket, if it's found."

"And?"

"She said she'd love to have it." He smiled up at Debbie. "I think we'll get it back, don't you?"

Debbie nodded. She hoped so, anyway.

Ray gestured toward the bench. "Do you have time to sit?"

"Yes. And I've brought you a gift." Debbie held up the jar of flowers.

"Aww." Ray smiled. "Mama's roses. And my forget-me-nots. Thank you."

Debbie held the jar so he could smell the flowers.

He inhaled deeply. "They're perfect."

Debbie placed the jar on the bench and then sat beside it. "Do you have time for a few questions?"

Ray closed the book and put it in his lap. "What do you need to know?"

"Did you know a woman named Isabella Adams when you were in England?"

Ray pursed his lips, humming in thought. Then he smiled. "Well, there was Izzy in Cornwall. She was the secretary for the Royal Engineers. Nice gal. Probably about my age."

"Izzy is often a nickname for Isabella, right?"

"Yes, although I never heard anyone call her Isabella. But that doesn't mean it wasn't her name."

"Were Izzy and Leland Clark close?"

"Leland would have liked to have been close with her."

"Even though he was dating Edith at the time and pining after Alié?"

Ray sighed. "It's hard to explain. I could say things were different back then, but I'm not sure if that's true. Clark must sound like a ladies' man to you. But people tended to date more then. Edith dated other men while Clark was in Cornwall. And it wasn't as if he dated Izzy, really. They went to a movie every so often. I know he asked her for her address before he left England so he could write to her. But he and I lost touch, so I don't know what became of that."

"Did you date any women while you were in England?"

"I truly had eyes only for Eleanor. I'd made my choice. Sergeant Clark hadn't made his. He was still playing the field, trying to find that special someone. From what I can tell, we were more casual in our dating habits than most are today. And, of course, people married younger." Ray clasped his book with both hands. "Why do you ask?"

"Leland Clark married Isabella Adams. She died in 2006."

Ray's face fell. "If he married Izzy, I would have liked to have seen her, along with Leland himself. I was always fond of Izzy." He chuckled. "I think out of the three, Edith, Alié, and Izzy, that Izzy was the best suited for him."

"Why is that?"

"She wasn't smitten with him."

"Neither was Alié."

Ray smiled wryly. "Actually, she was. She was playing hard to get."

"Really?"

"She wrote to me a few years after the end of the war and told me that Leland had stopped writing her and she regretted being coy with him." He chuckled again. "As for Izzy, she was a friend to all of us. Gave us good advice. Watched out for us. Made sure we received our packages and letters. She treated everyone with respect. She was tall with auburn hair and warm brown eyes. Most of the men were crazy about her, but she didn't pay much attention. Oh, she'd go out now and then, but it was obvious she wasn't looking to go steady with anyone. She had her little brother to care for."

"What else do you remember about Izzy?"

"She loved to read and loaned me a few books. Dickens. Thomas Hardy. Robert Louis Stevenson."

"Did she know you and Leland Clark were friends?"

"I'm not sure," he said. "I don't remember talking with her about Leland, and I have no idea what he might have said to her about me. There weren't a lot of American soldiers working with us. She would have probably assumed we were at least acquainted."

Debbie leaned back. "Do you have your records from the war?"

"I have my discharge documents and information about my medals."

"Does the information say why they were awarded?"

"No. Just general information."

"I was talking with Kim about Greg's grandfather because Greg doesn't know the circumstances of his death. She suggested checking the morning reports from his grandfather's platoon."

"Yes. The unit clerk submitted a morning report each day. Details about the location of the company, numbers, information about who had arrived and who had left, who went AWOL or MIA. Who was killed in action. Who was injured. Sometimes info about the weather. Encounters with the enemy. That sort of thing."

"So there would be information included in the morning report about when you were injured in the Netherlands?"

"Absolutely."

"Do you mind if I request the morning report for that day?"

"Not at all. I'd like to have you read through them. I doubt I need to though. I don't think I'd be surprised by anything in the reports, since I lived it."

"Great. Thank you. I just need the pertinent information." Debbie took out her phone and found her screenshot from the research she did for Greg. She read, "'The exact unit of assignment, a description of the action, and an approximate date.'"

"That's easy." He rattled off the information, and she wrote it down in her notes.

Debbie put her phone on the bench. "Do you know if the Royal Engineers did morning reports?"

"I'm sure they did some sort of regular report, but I don't know how you'd find the information."

"Do you think the information would have been shared with the US Army?"

"I have no idea," Ray said.

"Would you mind if I look into that too?"

"Of course not." Ray smiled. "Dig into whatever you want. You have my blessing." He rubbed his chin thoughtfully. "It's amazing how all those memories came flooding back once I opened myself up to them. I thought I'd moved past them, but here I am, circling around again."

"Is it painful?" Debbie asked.

"Not at all," Ray replied. "I'm not going over the battle memories again. This time it's about the people. Isn't it something how you can meet someone and think it's just a chance encounter, but then it ends up being so much more? I never expected that the memories of people like Anne, Alié, Izzy, and Edith would be the ones I'd keep and the images of the fighting and the injuries and the fear would fade. At the time it seemed like the opposite would be true."

Debbie reached forward and laid her hand on top of his as it rested on the book.

"I suppose that's a blessing," he said. "Or perhaps when memories are weighed through the test of time—eighty years, for example—those with the most value are the memories of the good people that I shared life with, even if it was only hours or days. Somehow those good memories outweigh the horrors of war caused by the bad people. For me, anyway."

"I'm glad." Debbie knew that many didn't have that blessing, that the horror often overshadowed the good memories Ray referred to.

Then he sighed. "Although I suppose it's not that simple. The bad had lasting consequences. I lost Eleanor because of the war. Millions and millions of people lost their lives. I don't think anyone in the world was unaffected."

"To say nothing of the subsequent generations," Debbie agreed, thinking of how her life and Greg's had been changed by the consequences of war.

Ray gave her a little smile. "I'll try to keep concentrating on the good, on the friends I made along the way." He reached for the bouquet of roses and forget-me-nots. "I planted the forget-me-nots from seed near Mama's roses when I first returned from the war. They grew and spread and reseeded. A few times over the years I planted more seed to give them a boost." He held the bouquet to his nose, directed toward the forget-me-nots. "They don't really have a smell, but since they grow so close to my mother's roses, I've always imagined they smelled like roses. That hasn't changed."

"Good."

He ran a finger over one flower. "I always felt they were as sweet as the friends I made all those years ago. I planted the forget-me-nots as a tribute to all of them, so that I'd never forget. And I haven't."

CHAPTER SIXTEEN

Wraxall, England
May 4, 1945

As Ray shook hands with his sergeant in the foyer of Edith's boardinghouse, he felt overwhelmed with gratitude that he and Sergeant Clark were both being sent to the English Channel. He'd feared they would be assigned to different locations.

Ray let go of Clark's hand and turned to the staircase. "Anne. Comment vas tu?"

"Much better," she answered in English. "How are you?"

"Fantastic," Ray said. "It's wonderful to be here with all of you. When does Alié arrive?"

"Any minute." Anne's English was perfect. "When you came in, I thought it was her until I saw you."

As if on cue, Alié called, "Bonjour!" through the open door.

Ray quickly welcomed her inside. As they all greeted each other, he felt the warmth of community, of young people from three different countries brought together during a worldwide war. He felt a camaraderie with his fellow soldiers, but he felt a deep sense of humanity with these friends.

Edith turned to Alié. "Anne has an appointment for her final examination in the morning. You won't be able to leave until after that, but you can stay here tonight."

"Thank you," Alié said.

"And you're all invited to dinner," Edith added. "The other boarders are working or gone for the evening. My landlady has agreed to make dinner for us. A final meal before you go your separate ways." She gave a sad smile. "I know you all need to go home or"—she glanced toward Ray and then Leland—"get closer to going home. But I certainly will miss you. Knowing you has been the best thing that could have happened to me, and it has really helped offset the awfulness going on everywhere else."

"I feel that way too," Sergeant Clark said, stepping forward and putting his arm around her.

Did Ray detect jealousy flashing across Alié's face? Before he could decide, she asked him, "Where are you and Leland going?"

"Guernsey," Ray answered. "To clear minefields set by the Germans."

She smiled. "You'll be closer to Paris." She turned her attention to Sergeant Clark. "Perhaps the two of you can get a pass to come visit." She pivoted toward Edith. "And you too. We won't have to say our forever goodbyes tomorrow."

"That would be lovely," Edith said. "Let's try to make that happen." It seemed Edith hadn't noticed the hint of jealousy on Alié's face. Perhaps Alié had been feigning interest in Ray to make Sergeant Clark jealous—and to stay in Edith's good favor. After all, Edith had cared for Anne when Alié couldn't.

Ray couldn't imagine he and Sergeant Clark would be able to go to Paris, but it was a nice thought. Although he'd much rather get home sooner and find out where Eleanor was than relax in France. His last letters to her had come back with Return to sender *stamped on them, and Gayle said no one in Dennison had heard from her.*

Alié stepped to the middle of the foyer and pointed to the living room. "Ray, look!"

Ray stepped beside her and spotted the upright piano.

Anne clapped her hands. "We can have music tonight."

"Dinner for the five of us and music," Sergeant Clark said. "What could be better?"

"Only the end of the war," Ray said.

"It will come soon." Sergeant Clark grinned. "Maybe even today."

"Within the next few days, for sure." Ray glanced around the group of friends. "We must stay in touch. Could we exchange addresses? Each one of you has helped me get through this war. I really don't want to lose touch with any of you."

"Hear, hear!" Sergeant Clark boomed. "Let's exchange addresses right now—our home addresses included."

With Edith's, Sergeant Clark's, and the Dumas family's addresses safely tucked in his jacket pocket, Ray sat with the others at the table. Edith's landlady, a widow named Mrs. Russell, had prepared beef bourguignon that was heavy on the gravy and egg noodles and light on the beef—but still delicious. She served roasted vegetables and fresh baked rolls alongside it and trifle for dessert.

Afterward, the young people helped clear the table and did the dishes while Mrs. Russell relaxed in the living room with a well-deserved cup of tea.

Then Ray took his place at the piano. Mrs. Russell joined them in singing for a while then excused herself. "Keep singing," she said. "I'll be down at nine to make sure the gentlemen have left."

At 8:55, Ray started playing "Down Forget-Me-Not Lane." Alié stood closest to the piano, and he could hear her clear voice as she sang about rainy days and rainbows. Ray realized a rainbow had come—to stay. The war in Europe would end soon. Of course, there was always the possibility of being sent to the Pacific if the war with Japan didn't end soon too, but hopefully it would. And then he'd be home.

The end was in sight.

After he played the last note, Alié gestured toward the piano. "I hope we'll always live on Forget-Me-Not Lane."

"Oh, I love that," Edith gushed. She glanced around the room. "I'll never forget any of you. Ever."

Ray felt the same way. "We'll be the Forget-Me-Not Club."

The others laughed, but Alié said, "That's a great idea." After a round of hugs, the young people said their goodbyes to each other.

"But this is only 'so long,'" Alié said. "We'll write. We'll keep in touch. We'll never forget."

"Absolutely," Ray agreed.

Alié and Anne returned to Paris the next day. On Sunday, Ray attended services at the church in Wraxall, and then early Monday morning, he and Sergeant Clark sat in the mess hall with Edith, who was working the night shift and had finally slipped away for a cup of coffee.

"So this is it," Edith said glumly. "You're off to Guernsey."

"After we go back to Cornwall," Sergeant Clark said. "We don't know the exact date we need to report to Guernsey yet."

Ray glanced at the clock at the end of the mess hall. He and Sergeant Clark had half an hour before they needed to catch the train for their last days in Cornwall. Ray was eager to move on to their next post.

Edith stood. "I need to get going."

As Ray rose to hug her goodbye, someone shouted, "Germany surrendered!"

All heads snapped toward where the voice came from. A British captain climbed up on a table. "It's over! Germany surrendered!"

"Who says?" someone shouted.

"It was on the radio," the captain shouted. "They signed the papers a few hours ago."

The powers that be must have stayed up half the night hashing out the details.

Clapping and shouts erupted throughout the mess hall. Ray hugged Edith again. She kissed his cheek and shouted over the racket, "Write to me."

"I will," Ray shouted back.

Then she turned and hugged Sergeant Clark. He kissed her, and then she pulled away and headed toward the exit, turning at the door to blow two kisses. Ray waved in return.

More soldiers climbed on tables. Sergeant Clark pushed Ray closer to the piano. "Play something."

Ray sat, set his hands on the keys, and began playing "God Save the King." Everyone sang along with gusto. When he finished, he launched into the "Star-Spangled Banner." He pounded away at the keys until it was time to leave.

Sergeant Clark spoke with a captain and then broke away from him to join Ray. As they hurried out of the mess hall, Sergeant Clark said, "We're to report at the dock in Poole by ten a.m. on Thursday. We'll ship to Guernsey then. I have a few more days of leave. I'll meet you there."

"You're not returning to Cornwall?"

"Not today. I'll swing back by to grab my things, but don't wait for me. I'll meet you in Poole."

"Okay," Ray said. "I'll see you then."

Sergeant Clark's eyes sparkled. "See you in three days."

Ray rode the train south, focusing on the English countryside as the sun rose. Emerald fields glittered with dew in the morning light. Lambs frolicked around the ewes. Union Jacks flew at every station. Passengers and waiters, civilians and other soldiers, all laughing in relief. Several people approached Ray and shook his hand, saying, "Thank you." One said, "Thanks be to God and you American soldiers."

"Thanks be to God." Ray fought back tears as relief flooded through him. Until he thought about clearing minefields on Guernsey. And the possibility of later being sent to the Pacific. He put those thoughts behind him. Today was a day to celebrate. Europe had been saved.

He would let tomorrow worry about itself.

CHAPTER SEVENTEEN

On Tuesday, Ray headed to the office to tell Izzy good-bye, but she wasn't there. A different young woman sat in her chair.

"I'm looking for Izzy," Ray said.

"She went home to Bodmin a few days ago," the woman said.

"When is she coming back?"

"She's not," the woman said. "Her home has been repaired, and she's secured a job there."

Ray thanked the woman and headed to his barracks, hoping Izzy and Timmy would have a good life back in their hometown now that the war was over.

On Thursday morning, as Ray waited to board at Poole Harbour with a group of Royal Engineers and a handful of American soldiers, he expected Sergeant Clark to show up any minute. It was a few minutes past ten. Where was he?

Finally, as the first of the engineers began to board, Sergeant Clark came running down the dock, his duffel bag bouncing on his back. Wearing a broad grin, he saluted the commanding officers then stepped to Ray's side. "Whew," he said. "I wasn't sure I was going to make it."

"Glad you did, Sarge," Ray said.

"Likewise. I left Suffolk Monday night, as soon as I collected my things, and took the overnight train to Bodmin. I arrived Tuesday morning, and then I took the train here last night but went to the wrong dock this morning. Thankfully, I figured it out in time."

Ray couldn't help but ask, "Why did you go to Bodmin?" Even though he knew the answer.

"To visit Izzy." He winked. "She and Timmy are both glad to be back home."

"That's good to hear," Ray said.

"She told me last week they were returning to their home. But you're the one who inspired me to visit her."

"I did?"

"Yes. Your little speech at Edith's boardinghouse about all of us staying in touch. I hadn't gotten Izzy's address, so I decided to go after it. She's someone I want to stay in touch with too."

"I'm glad." After the initial shock of Clark going to Bodmin, Ray's heart warmed. His friend had a gift

when it came to people. He genuinely seemed to enjoy connection with others. He was good at relationships. It would serve him well someday as a lawyer.

The boat ride across the channel to Guernsey was rough even though the sun was shining. Ray stood along the railing with his eyes on the horizon, wishing he could see land. He'd been seasick sailing from New York to England and had spent as much time on deck as possible. He'd do the same now.

Around noon, the crew passed out sandwiches and tea. Ray's stomach rolled at the idea of food. Sergeant Clark held out his hand. "I'll take yours," he said. Ray gave it to him and sipped the tea.

Nearly seven hours into the trip, he spotted land. "Is that Guernsey?" he asked.

"No," an engineer on the other side of him answered. "That's France. We have another hour to Guernsey." He smiled. "It's much smaller than the mainland."

Ray tried to laugh, but a groan came out instead.

"Hold tight," the engineer said. "We'll arrive at St. Peter Port before you know it."

The afternoon sun sparkled on the water as the wind whipped against Ray's face. He searched the deck for Sergeant Clark. He finally saw him sitting on a bench, talking with another soldier. He didn't appear to be bothered by seasickness at all. In so many ways, especially now that they were off the front, Clark came off like a golden boy again. Nearly everything seemed to come easily to him.

At long last, more land came into view. "There it is," the engineer said. "We'll be docked in no time."

A harbor with a picturesque town—white stucco buildings with church steeples and spires rising behind them—came into view. St. Peter Port was a good-sized town. South of the harbor was a castle with a light-house on the pier in front of it. Ahead was a crowd on one of the docks.

"Nazis," the engineer said under his breath.

Ray's stomach flipped. "Seriously?"

"That group is most likely being relocated, proba-bly to POW camps in France. Some will stay and be forced to help clear the minefields, which is only fair, since they set them."

Ray hadn't expected to be required to work with Nazis. His wounded leg began to ache, most likely from standing for so long. The boat slowed. As it docked, lurching to the right, Ray's stomach flipped again.

The Nazis on the dock turned toward the boat. They wore faded uniforms and rusted helmets. All were thin. It didn't appear that life had been easy on Guernsey for them, and no doubt it had been worse for the citizens of the island.

Trying to take his mind off his stomach, Ray asked the engineer, "Can you tell me how Guernsey is connected to England?"

"It's a little complicated," the engineer answered. "It's a self-governing island but a Crown Dependency and British-owned. It's officially known as the Bailiwick of Guernsey, which includes a few other islands."

"Interesting." Ray had no idea such entities existed.

"March!" a British soldier barked, and the Nazi soldiers started up the gangplank.

"Do you see those men over there?" The engineer pointed toward the castle. On the very last dock, a group of men sat on crates. They were dressed mostly in rags, some with blankets draped over their shoulders. A few began boarding a boat.

"Yes," Ray said.

"Laborers," the engineer said. "Forced laborers. Algerians. Poles. Russians. Jews. Dissenters. All captured by the Germans. They were barely cared for, much like the civilians. If it hadn't been for a Red Cross ship from Portugal with food and other supplies making half a dozen or so visits here, many would have starved to death."

Ray shivered. "How do you know?"

"There was a clandestine radio operator sending out information about the Germans on Guernsey for most of the war. He went silent two weeks ago. Most likely captured."

Ray shivered again and hoped the engineer didn't notice.

"The Germans on the island surrendered yesterday," the engineer said. "No doubt, in the weeks to come, we'll see the horrific suffering that's gone on here."

"No doubt," Ray managed to say.

Ray knew the only British territory the Germans occupied during World War II were four of the Channel Islands—Guernsey, Alderney, Sark, and Jersey. Hitler had hoped they'd be jumping-off points to invade Britain.

As the engineers and soldiers reached the first street, townspeople greeted them, waving Union Jacks, clapping and shouting. A young woman from a second-floor window yelled, "Americans too? Thank you!"

Sergeant Clark waved at her, and she blew him a kiss.

Along the street, some British soldiers stood guard while others escorted more German soldiers toward the dock.

The Royal Engineers and American soldiers fell into formation and marched up the hill, past the church *and finally past the edge of town. They stopped at a bunker that had recently been vacated by the Germans.*

"Clean it out," someone called. "We have rations for supper. A kitchen will be set up by morning."

That night Ray fell asleep on a concrete floor, but he couldn't complain. It was dry and bearable inside his military-issued wool sleeping bag.

The next morning, after a breakfast of porridge and tea, the engineers and soldiers met with German engineers and then divided into two groups. One went to a nearby beach while the other, including Ray and Sergeant Clark, went up the road to where anti-tank mines had been planted. It seemed ridiculous to mine roads on the island, but the Germans had feared that the Allies might attack during the Normandy invasion or after.

The American soldiers started out patrolling the road to ensure that civilians didn't get in the way of the engineers. As Ray was at the far end of the road, a girl—probably around ten—came out of the trees with an older woman. The girl wore a dress that was too short for her, a sweater with patched elbows, and worn shoes. Her brown hair was braided. The woman, who Ray guessed might be her grandmother, wore a worn coat and boots.

The woman stayed at the edge of the trees while the girl approached Ray. "Is it really safe now?"

Ray put out his hand to stop her. "No, it's not. The engineers are dismantling the mines."

She glanced up the road. "But they're British, right?"

"Yes," Ray answered.

"What are you?"

"American."

"So the Germans are really gone?"

"The occupation is over. Some of the Germans have stayed to help clear the minefields."

"What about the laborers?"

"I'm not sure. Some are being shipped away to England," Ray said. "I imagine others are receiving care."

The girl stepped toward the woman and motioned to her. The woman moved back into the trees and then returned with another person at her side. Ray took a step closer to the girl and the woman and the other person, who, on closer look, was a man dressed in a baggy pair of pants and a shirt with a tear in the side. He wore shoes held together with twine. When he saw Ray, the man stopped.

"It's all right, Ivan," the girl said to the man. "He's American. You can come out."

The man shuffled forward.

"Hello," Ray said.

Ivan nodded an acknowledgment.

"I'm Adele Martin," the girl said. "This is my grandmother."

The woman extended her hand. "Jeanne Martin." She gestured toward the man. "And this is Ivan."

"He's a Russian laborer who has been hiding from the Germans." Adele smiled at the man. "We've been helping him."

"What does Ivan need?" Ray asked.

"Food," Jeanne said. "Medical care for the cut on his foot and for the rash on his arm."

"All right. The three of you wait here. I'll find out where the laborers are getting assistance."

After conferring with Sergeant Clark and then the engineer he'd spoken with on the boat, Ray determined that Town Church was where Ivan should go.

"Go with them," Sergeant Clark said. "I can guard the road by myself."

As Ray led them along a path that was clear of mines, he took a chocolate bar from his pocket and handed it to Adele. "Split this between the three of you."

Jeanne said, "I don't care for any, but thank you. Adele, split it in two for you and Ivan."

The girl did as her grandmother instructed.

Adele ate the chocolate quickly while Ivan took small bites. When Adele finished, she asked, "Where are you from?"

"Ohio," Ray answered. "A little town called Dennison."

She skipped a few steps. "Do you miss your family?"

"Yes, very much so."

"I miss my mum. And my dad. But he may be coming home soon."

Ray concentrated on asking about her father, fearing something had happened to her mother. "Where has he been?"

"Off fighting since 1939." She reached for Jeanne's hand. "I live with Granny. We'll all live together when Dad returns."

"I hope that will be soon," Ray said.

"So do I. It should be any day now." Adele let go of her grandmother's hand and started to skip ahead.

"Stay behind me, Adele," Ray said. "Just to be safe."

She froze.

Ray passed her. "You can direct me to the church. Make sure and tell me to turn left or right when we reach the street."

"Right," she told him a few minutes later.

At the church, a British medic treated Ivan's cut and rash. Then a Red Cross volunteer handed each of them a cup of soup and a piece of bread.

Ray watched them eat. Again, Adele consumed the food quickly while Ivan savored each bite. Jeanne took a few bites and then handed her cup of soup to Adele and her piece of bread to Ivan.

A man behind Ray said to the woman next to him, "Do you think Delpha will return?"

"Hush," the woman said.

"She could have continued being a mother to her daughter, but she threw that away to hide a Russian laborer. I'll never understand it," the man said. "She's probably in one of those German camps we've heard about—if she's alive at all. She must have known she'd never get away with it. What was she thinking?"

Ray realized they were talking about Adele's mother and took a step to the side, hoping to block Adele's view of the man and woman.

"It's called conviction," the woman hissed. "It's called loving your neighbor as yourself."

"Well, it's one thing to love your neighbor as yourself. But no one should love their neighbor more than their child—a child that stayed on the island instead of being sent to safety with the others. And now, it appears little Adele, with Jeanne's help, has been caring for

the Russian. They're lucky they weren't caught and sent off to a camp too."

"Stop," the woman said.

The man was silent for a moment and then said, "And I heard Harold was captured for operating an illegal radio." Ray thought of the radio operator the engineer had mentioned when they arrived in the St. Peter Port harbor.

"Stop talking," the woman said again. "It's enough that Jeanne has lost her daughter-in-law and now Harold. You don't need to be gossiping about it."

Ray turned his head toward the thud of boots on the stone floor. The man, who looked to be about in his early forties, walked to the exit with his arms crossed.

The woman approached Jeanne and said, "It's good to see you in town. How are you doing?"

"Just fine," Jeanne answered, raising her chin and squaring her shoulders. "I thank you for asking."

Adele started to say something, but Jeanne quickly put her finger to her lips.

The woman said, "Bless you all," and walked away.

After Adele and her grandmother finished their soup, they told Ivan goodbye. The grandmother hugged him and then Adele did too. He clung to them and swiped at his eyes as he said, "Thank you" over and over again.

Ray offered to walk Adele and her grandmother back to the road.

"That's not necessary," Jeanne assured him. "I need to ask around about whether my son will be coming home soon."

"Where was he stationed when he was injured?"

"The last letter we got said he was in a hospital in France, recovering. He hoped he'd be home as soon as the war was over." Jeanne pushed a stray hair from her face. "And Adele wants to find out when her friends will return from England. It's been a long time since she's had anyone to play with."

Adele crossed her arms. "I barely remember these children Granny calls my friends. I haven't minded being without other children. I'm very grateful my mum didn't send me away. Most of the other children had to leave."

"Yes," Jeanne said. "I'm grateful she didn't send you away too." She patted her granddaughter's head. "Come along. Let's see if we've had a letter from your father."

Ray walked out of the church with them and then watched as they made their way down the cobblestone street. Heroes came in all sizes and ages. He said a prayer that Adele would indeed be united with her father.

Even though it was now the beginning of June, the days were chilly on Guernsey and the nights in the bunker were downright cold with the rain and wind coming off the ocean and the resulting unrelenting dampness.

Ray hummed hymns as he cleared mines on roads, in the forest, and on beaches, kept civilians safe, and monitored the German captives. One engineer was injured when a mine detonated as he approached it. Shrapnel tore through his right arm, sending him to the ground. Ray rushed forward and applied a tourniquet. The medic arrived quickly, and then the engineer was transported to the town for medical care. He'd be transferred to England as soon as possible. Later that evening the medic told Ray the tourniquet had likely saved the man's life—although he'd no doubt lose the arm.

Sergeant Clark retreated when the engineer was injured. That evening back at the barracks, he didn't seem to be his usual, cheerful self.

"How are you doing?" Ray asked him when the medic left.

"Just feeling a little melancholy," Sergeant Clark replied. "Ready to go home, I guess."

The next week, Clark and Ray had a day off and went into town in the afternoon. They stopped for tea, *and as the waitress served them, a girl popped into the café. It was Adele.*

Ray waved at her, which made her smile. Then he gestured for her to join them. She approached the table and said, "I'm looking for Granny. Have you seen her?"

Before Ray could answer, Jeanne came into the café. She looked around, and when she saw them, she said, "Adele. There you are. Hello," she added to Ray and Sergeant Clark. "How are the two of you doing this afternoon?"

"Good." Clark seemed to be back to normal. "How are the two of you?"

"Oh, we can't complain." Jeanne held up an envelope. "In fact, we have some good news." She put her hand on Adele's shoulder. "We got a letter from your father. He believes he'll be home by the end of this week."

Adele beamed. "Do you think he'll come on the ferry?"

"Probably." Jeanne smiled. "I doubt the army would set up a separate transport for him."

Three days later, Ray was back on the road above town, guarding a field that the engineers were clearing of mines. Adele came out of the trees and walked toward him. "I'm going down to meet the ferry," she called out. "I hope my father is on it."

Ray waved. "I hope he is too."

An hour later, Adele trudged up the road from the village, holding a baguette in her hand.

"Aw," Ray said as she approached him. "I take it he wasn't on the ferry."

She shook her head. "I met the ferry yesterday too, and he wasn't on it then either."

"Perhaps tomorrow."

"I hope so," she said.

"How is your grandmother?"

"She's not feeling well." Adele held up the baguette. "She's home resting. She let me buy this for our dinner."

Ray hoped they had more than the bread to eat. He pulled a chocolate bar from the pocket of his jacket. "Take this too."

Her eyes lit up. "Thank you."

Sergeant Clark waved at Adele from down the road. "Tell your grandmother hello from us."

Adele waved back. "I will."

Sergeant Clark wasn't talking much and still seemed to be dwelling on the engineer who had lost his arm. Ray decided that it made sense that Sergeant Clark's mood fluctuated depending on the threat level. Ray knew how easy it was to fall into despair, but he trusted in the Lord. Since France, he still woke up every morning thanking God for a new day. He hoped he never stopped.

For Ray, the biggest blessing of serving on Guernsey had been meeting Jeanne and Adele. And there were many other blessings too. Getting to know the Royal Engineers. Protecting civilians from the land mines. Watching the Germans help dismantle what had been meant for harm. But Ray couldn't help thinking about what danger they were still in too. The war wasn't over for them—not yet.

The next day, Ray and Sergeant Clark guarded the field again. Ray expected Adele to come by at the same time as she had the day before, shortly before noon. When she didn't appear, he guessed she'd taken a different route. The day was bright and sunny. He patrolled the road with Sergeant Clark and two other US soldiers while the engineers worked.

A little after noon the Royal Engineers, the German engineer working with them, and the two other Americans headed to the bunker for lunch. Sergeant Clark and Ray stood guard, leaning against the fence around the field, in the shadow of a tree.

"This is more dangerous than I thought it would be," Sergeant Clark said. "Do you think the engineer who got his arm blown off really did survive?"

"Yes," Ray said. "He's getting good care in England."

"I don't see why they need us," Sergeant Clark said. "Brits could be doing this. Anyone could be doing this."

Ray heard a rustling and turned to look at the far end of the field. Adele was running toward the fence.

"Adele!" Ray called out. "Stop!"

Wind blew through the treetops, and perhaps she couldn't hear him. She scrambled over the fence. The engineers had been dismantling the last remaining mine in the middle of the field, and Adele was headed straight for it.

"Adele!" Ray dropped his rifle and climbed over the fence.

Sergeant Clark yelled something, but Ray ignored him.

Ray ran at an angle to intercept Adele. Their point of intersection was where the engineers had been working.

"Stop!" he yelled again.

Adele didn't stop. In fact, she ran faster.

She couldn't hear him. Ray had to get to her. Before the unthinkable happened.

CHAPTER EIGHTEEN

When Debbie got home from Good Shepherd, she called Jonathon. He answered on the first ring. "Hello, Debbie. Have you found the jacket?"

"No," she answered. "But I did have an interesting conversation with Heather Clark."

"Really? What did she have to say?"

"A couple of things," Debbie answered. "One, that she was interested for a short time in buying a Purple Heart you were selling on your website."

"She was?"

"Yes. I knew you collected World War II items, but I had no idea you sold them as well."

He chuckled. "Well, that's the thing with collecting. If you don't also sell, you're a hoarder. My online business is a great way for me to pare down my collection. It started out as a hobby. It got me traveling around the US and then Europe too. But I don't have room to keep everything I find. I like to think that selling some of my collection is helping people who can't do the traveling themselves have a part of history. It's still just a hobby though. I don't make nearly enough from what I sell to cover the cost of obtaining them, and because some people object, I usually don't talk about it."

That must have been why he'd lied to Cassie about the call he'd gotten during their meeting. Debbie didn't have a problem with people collecting war memorabilia. After all, that was what Kim did at the museum. But she wasn't sure how she felt about people buying and selling Purple Hearts and other medals of honor for profit. Jonathon apparently didn't have any trouble with the idea, and she wouldn't judge his choices. She simply found it odd that he hadn't disclosed that he both collected and sold World War II memorabilia, including jackets like Ray's.

Jonathon asked, "Are you still there?"

"Yes," she answered. "The other thing Heather said is that you agree with her that Ray stole her father's story about saving Adele Martin's life on Guernsey. I know you thought the story could belong to either of the two men, but why would you say that to Heather? Especially without evidence?"

"I don't think I did," he said.

"She thinks you did."

"Well, Heather Clark thinks all sorts of things."

"Such as?"

"That her father was the best politician the state ever had. That if he had run, he could have become a US senator, and after that, the president."

"Really?"

"You bet. Ask her about it sometime."

"Did you know Leland Clark?"

"Of course. Everyone who was alive during his tenure in the Ohio General Assembly knew Leland Clark."

Debbie told Jonathon about Ray writing Leland once he'd been elected and then leaving a message for him. "But Ray never heard back from him."

"Leland must not have received the letter or the phone message. Blame it on his staff," Jonathon said. "He always answered correspondence and returned calls. He was the most dependable person I knew when it came to maintaining connections. He was made to be a politician. It's really a shame that he didn't get the letter or phone call. That would have been some reunion."

Debbie didn't respond.

"Then again, perhaps Ray merely claimed that he sent the letter and left the message. Perhaps he didn't want to have contact because he'd told the story as his own."

"Had he?" Debbie asked. "I didn't know that story until Oliver Godfrey told it last week. Ray never mentioned it to me."

"Then let me play devil's advocate. Why wouldn't he have? Why would he keep that a secret?"

"There's no evidence he kept it secret. But my guess is he didn't talk about it because he didn't want to sound as if he was bragging." Debbie paused. "Wait a minute. Maybe he told Gayle—his sister— about the rescue. I'll find out and let you know."

"That's not necessary," Jonathon said.

"No, it actually is," Debbie insisted. "I'll call you right back."

Gayle answered on the second ring. "Is Ray all right?"

"Yes," Debbie said. "I didn't mean to scare you."

"Did you find the jacket?"

"Not yet. I'm actually calling to ask if you knew about Ray rescuing Adele Martin. Did he tell you when he returned home?"

"I'm sure he told our folks. I remember one night coming down to get a drink of water after bedtime, and the three of them were sitting around the kitchen table. Mom was crying and said, 'To think you saved that girl's life.' But that was all I heard. They stopped talking when I came into the room. That must have been what he was talking about."

"It sounds likely," Debbie agreed.

"You'd think he would have told me. The next morning I told him what I'd heard and asked him what it was all about, but he said it was nothing and I should forget it. Honestly, Ray didn't talk about the war at all with me until he was in his sixties. I think he wanted to protect me. I think that was pretty common of World War II vets—of a lot of vets. Why do you ask?"

Debbie told Gayle about her conversation with Heather and then with Jonathon.

Gayle gasped. "They think Ray stole Leland Clark's story? That Oliver Godfrey is confused and that Ray is lying?"

"Heather appears to think that. Jonathon too."

Gayle's voice rose. "You know, I was never that impressed with Leland Clark when he was interviewed on TV. He seemed a little too slick. And I'm not thinking too kindly of Heather right now either."

Debbie suddenly wasn't sure calling Gayle had been the smart thing to do. "I didn't mean to upset you."

"No, I'm glad you told me. Ray would never pick up the phone and give me this information. He wouldn't want to worry me. Thank you so much for calling. I need to know when someone is accusing my brother of lying."

"You've been helpful," Debbie said. "Thank you."

Debbie called Jonathon back, but he didn't pick up. She left a message, saying, "Gayle, Ray's younger sister, remembers that he saved a girl's life while overseas, but he never told her the details. Please return my call when you can."

About a half hour later Debbie's doorbell rang. She was surprised to see Janet standing on her front porch.

"Do you have a minute?" Janet asked.

"Of course," Debbie said. "How about a glass of lemonade?"

"Sure." Janet gestured to Debbie's roses. "Those are lovelier than ever."

"Well, probably not than ever." Debbie laughed. "But lovelier than last year. I think I'm getting the hang of gardening." She noted that the forget-me-nots were beginning to fade. But they'd be back in their full glory next year.

"What's up?" Debbie asked as Janet stepped into the house.

"Two things." Janet followed Debbie into the kitchen. "First of all, Ian stopped by the house for tea. He had a phone call while he was there. I can tell you about it because it's not linked to an individual suspect. It's just general information."

"I'm all ears." Debbie took the pitcher of lemonade from the refrigerator.

Janet continued. "The phone call was about the make of shoe from the print, which you already know is a men's size ten."

Debbie nodded as she poured the lemonade.

"The shoe turned out to be a climbing shoe, made by a popular brand."

"I'm afraid I'm not well-versed in climbing shoes." Debbie handed Janet a glass and led the way out to the porch.

"Neither am I," Janet said. "But apparently they're a specialty shoe, used for rock climbing."

Debbie shook her head. "Maybe whoever was wearing the shoe bought it because they liked its design rather than because of how they planned to use it to climb through a window."

Janet nodded. "Yes," she said slowly. "But it makes sense that someone who climbs could get inside the dry cleaners through the window."

"That's true," Debbie said.

Janet swiped on her phone and then held it out to Debbie. "Here's a picture."

It was of a green shoe that appeared very flexible with a black rubber bottom. "I've never seen a shoe like this in my life."

"Neither have I," Janet said. "Keep an eye out for it though." She laughed. "Well, for two of them."

Debbie laughed too. "We'll be noticing every pair of shoes that comes into the café now." She took a sip of lemonade. "Anything else?"

Janet tucked a strand of hair behind her ear. "It turns out Tiffany has a friend who knows Ruby Clark from Ohio State. They're in the same sorority."

"What year is Ruby?"

"She'll be a senior."

"That's older than I thought. I wasn't exactly sure, but I'd placed her a couple years younger than that."

"I agree, she does look younger. Anyway, Tiffany asked her friend about Ruby. Her friend said that Ruby was pressured to join the sorority by her aunt, who belonged to the same one way back when. She said Ruby hardly makes a move without consulting her aunt."

"Does she have any other aunts besides Heather?"

"Not that I know of," Janet said. "But I don't know if we can say for sure that Ruby is trying to please Heather. She could be thinking that her connection to a state representative and the connections she's making in the sorority will get her a better job in the long run."

"What's she majoring in?"

"Political science. She plans to go to law school."

"Because she wants to or because Heather wants her to?" Debbie asked.

"I don't know," Janet answered.

"What about Ruby's mom? Is she in the picture?"

"Not much. Ruby's parents split when she was little. Her mom lives in Philadelphia, and her father raised her."

"It sounds as if Heather has filled a void in Ruby's life with her mother not living close by," Debbie said.

"I got that impression as well. Her mom is the CEO of a cosmetics company, so she's very successful. Ruby told Tiffany's friend that her father went to law school and then decided to teach instead. She said that's what caused the breakup of her parents' marriage. Her mom wanted a lawyer for a husband, not a teacher."

"Ouch. I wonder if his family was disappointed in him too."

After Janet left, Debbie decided to see about ordering the morning reports for Ray. If Greg hadn't already ordered the ones for his grandfather, maybe they could do it at the same time. She sent him a quick text.

LET'S WORK ON THEM TOGETHER, Greg texted back. I KEEP GET-TING DISTRACTED. COME OVER THIS EVENING IF YOU CAN.

Debbie sent him a thumbs-up emoji and got busy making her supper.

An hour later, as Debbie walked over to Greg's with her laptop, she got a text from Betsy.

I'M IN AKRON FOR A WEEK OR SO. I'LL TOUCH BASE IN A DAY OR TWO AND LET YOU KNOW MY SCHEDULE. I CAN COME YOUR WAY.

Debbie texted back, I'D LOVE TO SEE YOU. LET ME KNOW WHEN IT WILL WORK FOR YOU TO COME DOWN. WE CAN DO LUNCH AT THE CAFÉ.

When Debbie arrived at Greg's, Jaxon and Julian were shooting hoops.

"Dad's in the dining room," Julian called out. Then he executed a perfect hook shot.

"Thanks. Nice shot, by the way." She waved at Jaxon and headed to the back porch. When she opened the door, she called out, "Hello? It's me!"

"Come on in," Greg called.

She stepped through the kitchen with its slate floor, quartz counters, and massive island. Greg did good work.

He met her at the doorway to the dining room and gave her a hug. "Thank you for coming over."

They sat at the table side by side with their laptops and pulled up the website Kim had given them.

"I'm going to fill out a request for Ray's morning report from when he was injured in the Netherlands and the one from the day he was injured on Guernsey," Debbie said.

Greg watched her as she navigated through the process. Then they did the same on his computer with his grandfather's information.

After he submitted his request, Greg said, "Thank you. I really appreciate your help."

Debbie smiled at him. "I didn't do anything."

"Actually, you did. You coming over here and sitting down with me was the motivation I needed to get it done. With the boys' schedules and my work, I just wasn't taking the time to stop and do it."

She took his hand. "That's understandable. I'm glad we both had time for it tonight."

Greg nodded and squeezed her hand. "I've been thinking about the memories I have of my grandmother. She lived with us on the farm for three years after her second husband passed away. She was seventy or so and had a dog, several cats, and enough chickens to supply fresh eggs for the family. Mom and I helped her plant a garden every year. We tried to keep it small, but she kept making it bigger. She believed in growing her own instead of getting 'second-rate' vegetables at the store." He smiled. "She was really something. Back then, I didn't realize how remarkable she was and what a hard worker she'd been her entire life."

"Do you have any pictures of her?"

"I do. Mom put an album together for me. I'll get it." He disappeared into the living room and came back with a scrapbook. "Mom went through a major scrapbooking phase when I was in grade school."

Debbie chuckled. "She got the bug early then," she said. "I remember when scrapbooking was a huge thing about twenty years ago. My mom went crazy, with all the stickers and stencils."

He opened the album. "This one is entirely about Grandma. Mom made it for her and then gave it to me a few years ago." There was a black-and-white photo of his grandmother, Vivian, as a toddler, standing next to a rocking chair. Then one of her as a ten-year-old or so.

"We don't have a lot of pictures of her before she was married," Greg said. "I don't think they took many during her childhood."

"That's pretty common for back then," Debbie said. "She grew up during the Depression. Not everyone had cameras, and it was expensive to get film developed when you were trying to keep everyone fed."

Greg nodded. "That's true. And she was down the line in birth order, so you know how that goes. There's plenty of pictures of the oldest one, and then fewer and fewer of the others as the years go on." He pointed to a photo of his grandmother wearing a cap and gown. "That was her high school graduation." He pointed to the next photo. "That's my grandmother and grandfather on their wedding day. They married a week after she graduated."

Vivian wore a light-colored dress and a small hat with a veil. Earl Sr. wore a dark suit. Both smiled brightly. "They seem really happy," Debbie said.

"Don't they?" He straightened the photo in the book. "Everyone said they were madly in love. I'm happy she found love again with her second husband."

"I am too."

The next pages of photos were of the couple with one child, then two, then three. The last one was of the little family in front of a farmhouse with fields on both sides. "She was pregnant with my dad here," Greg said.

He turned the page. There was a photo of his grandfather in his uniform and another of him in front of the Dennison Depot. "This is the photo that made me so interested in World War II."

The next photo was of Vivian and a baby.

"That's my dad, Earl Jr.," Greg said.

"It must have been so hectic, taking care of three little kids, running a farm, and then having a fourth baby, all while her husband was gone," Debbie said. "I can't imagine what it was like when she found out he'd been killed."

Greg exhaled and then leaned toward her. "You can imagine better than most."

Debbie touched his arm. "So can you."

Greg squeezed her hand and turned to the next page. There were a couple of photos of Vivian and the kids, and then one of them with another man—Ted, Vivian's second husband. Debbie knew that Ted had served with Earl Sr. and had come to check on Vivian and the kids after the war. He was from Chicago and stopped in Dennison on his way home.

He'd ended up staying. First to help with the farm and then because he and Vivian fell in love. They had three more children, which the photographs showed. She knew from Greg's and Paulette's stories that Earl Jr. had grown up in a large, happy family.

"It's a shame my dad never knew his dad," Greg murmured. "His oldest sister had memories of him. His other two older sisters don't, but they have photographs of him with them. I think it was hard for my father not to have either of those things—no memories, and no photographs where his father was holding him. But I know he was loved. He had a close relationship with both his mom and Ted. Ted was the only father he ever knew, and he was a good one."

The other pages of photos showed Vivian with her children as they graduated and then with grandchildren. "That's me." Greg pointed to a color photo of Vivian sitting at a picnic table holding a sleeping newborn. Her smile lit up her entire face. "She loved being a grandma."

"I can tell," Debbie said. "I love that picture."

"So do I." Greg closed the album. "That's all for this album so far. I think Mom still has some photos she wants to add to it." After Greg's father died, Paulette moved out of their big family home and into a two-bedroom house. Some of her things were still in storage.

"Thank you," Debbie said. "I enjoyed seeing those."

There was a commotion at the back door. "I won!" Jaxon crowed.

"No you didn't," Julian shouted. "You cheated."

"Use your inside voice," Jaxon said mockingly.

Greg pushed the album toward the middle of the table and stood. "Hey, guys." He started into the kitchen. "Did you roll the bins to the curb?"

Julian groaned. "We forgot."

Jaxon yelled, "Race you!" The back door slammed once and then a second time.

Greg grinned. "And that's how a seasoned parent defuses a brewing argument."

Debbie laughed. "Whatever it takes." She slid her laptop into her backpack and stood. "I need to get going."

"Are you sure?"

She nodded. "I need to get ready for tomorrow—and put my own bins on the curb."

He gave her a hug. "I could send the boys over."

"Nah, I've got it. Hopefully, we'll get the information soon."

"I hope so," Greg said. "And if not, finding out where my grandfather is buried, going through the process of requesting more information, and showing you the pictures of him and Grandma has been helpful. It's good for me to think about Grandma from an adult perspective. Her resilience encourages me."

Debbie smiled. Vivian's story had encouraged her too.

CHAPTER NINETEEN

The next morning, Debbie had an email from an Evelyn Lewis. It read:

April Edwards gave me your name and email address. She said you were looking for information about Adele Martin Harris and Oliver Godfrey. I've been a member of the Isle of Guernsey Society for the last fifty years and knew Oliver Godfrey as a child. His mother was Adele Martin. She married John Godfrey, who died in a maritime accident when Oliver was around six. She remarried Matthew Harris a few years later, and they had two girls.

Oliver left the island while his sisters were still small. One sister left Guernsey in her late teens, and the other left after Adele died, around twenty years ago. I know Oliver came home to help care for their mother before she died. I saw him around town and said hello once and caught up a little. At that time he lived in Edinburgh. I haven't seen him since. I know one sister is in Ireland but have no idea where the other one is.

I do know that Oliver is a good person. He deeply loved his mother and his sisters. He was quiet and kind and caring. I hope this helps.

Debbie read the email again. *Quiet and kind and caring.* The person Evelyn Lewis knew didn't sound like someone who would crawl through a window and steal a World War II veteran's jacket. Her own parents, in the interaction they had with him at Ray's ceremony, felt Oliver was a dependable person too. And Debbie didn't have any red flags from interacting with him either.

She sighed. Of course, no one could truly know what another person was capable of after a brief interaction or from knowing them as a child. Sometimes it was hard to know someone, even if you lived with them and saw them every day. Hopefully Officer Jones would find some information there on Guernsey that would be helpful.

As she walked to work, her phone rang. *Jonathon.* She accepted the call.

"Good morning, Debbie. Sorry it took me a while to get back to you. I've been swamped."

"Hi, Jonathon."

"I listened to your message, but I've forgotten the details. Remind me what you needed to know?"

"I told you that Gayle, who is Ray's younger sister, remembers that he saved a girl's life when he was overseas. She overheard him talking with their parents about it."

"So?"

"So, you asked before if Ray had told anyone who was still living. He didn't tell Gayle directly, but she overheard him talking about it."

"Eighty years ago?" he asked pointedly.

"Neither one of them has memory problems."

"That doesn't prove anything."

"Yes, it does," Debbie said. "Gayle corroborated Ray's story."

"Not any more than Heather corroborated Leland's."

"Gayle overheard Ray's story long before Leland first told his story."

"Keep digging," Jonathon advised her. "And let me know what you find."

"Have you been digging?" Debbie demanded. "Have you been investigating Leland Clark's other assertions? And Heather's desire to have a Purple Heart for her father?"

"I don't have time. Besides, Heather didn't buy the Purple Heart from me. Just because she thinks her father should have gotten one doesn't mean she'd stoop to stealing one from another veteran."

"I hope she wouldn't," Debbie said. "I hope no one who was at Ray's ceremony would do that."

Jonathon huffed. "If you're thinking that I would do something like that, you can think again. Besides, there's no way I could have squeezed through that window."

Debbie reached the depot and sat down on a bench near the train tracks.

When she didn't answer, Jonathon said, "I wear a size twelve, and apparently the shoe print was from a size ten. I already spoke with Ian Shaw about the incident. In fact, I think he cleared me. You should ask him."

"When did you talk to him?"

"Yesterday. That's one of the reasons I didn't return your call. I wanted to wait until I spoke with Ian."

"He called you?"

"No, I drove to Dennison yesterday and spoke with him in person. I get that I come off looking suspicious in all of this. I wanted to clear my name," Jonathon said. "Plenty of celebrities—if you can call me that, perhaps a local celebrity anyway—do stupid things. But not me. I always think about what the consequences will be when it comes to the types of stories I choose, who I spend time with, and what I do with my hobby that's kind of a business. I've seen what happens to people in the public eye who act unethically. Anyone can be caught, and no one is immune. I told Ian I'd take a lie detector test or whatever else would clear my name. I would never steal from a veteran—or anyone else for that matter."

"Did you take a lie detector test?"

"No," Jonathon said. "Ian said it wasn't necessary."

"All right," Debbie said. "Did you get any responses to the interview with Ray?"

"No," Jonathon said. "Believe me, I'd call you even if it was the middle of the night if I did. I want that jacket to show up for Ray probably as much as you do. I started collecting World War II artifacts because I appreciate veterans. I admire what they've done for our country."

Despite her earlier suspicions, Debbie believed him. Unfortunately, that left her back at square one.

The morning progressed quickly. At ten thirty, Greg stopped by the café for a latte. As she served him, he said, "Have you checked your email? I have one from the National Archives."

Debbie put his latte on the counter. "Wow, that was fast."

He agreed. "They wanted me to call their office. When I did, the staff person handling my request said they don't get many requests from relatives or friends of World War II vets anymore. Most of the World War II requests are from people writing books or doing academic research. I told her about your request, and she said she was working on that too. She had extra time this morning, so she was able to expedite our cases."

"Nice," Debbie said.

"Yeah. There's a fee for expediting them, though. I was able to pay for my request, but she said since your name was on the other one, you'd have to pay the fee yourself if you want yours fast-tracked."

Debbie wiped her hands on her apron and took her phone out of her pocket. "Let me find the email...there it is. I'll do that right now." She was done in less than a minute. "There. All done."

Greg smiled and wrapped his hands around his to-go cup. "The archivist said she'd put the morning reports in the mail today. She said we might have the information as soon as Monday. I hope so. You need Ray's information sooner than I need my grandfather's."

During the noon rush, Debbie was in the middle of taking an order when her phone buzzed in her apron pocket. Hopefully, if it was important, whoever was calling would leave a message.

It wasn't until after closing that she was able to check her phone. Besides a voice mail, she had a text from Thom. MY WIFE AND DAUGHTER ARE IN COLUMBUS AND WOULD LOVE TO MEET YOU. COULD WE COME TO THE CAFÉ IN THE MORNING?

Debbie texted back at once. I'D LOVE TO MEET YOUR FAMILY AND SEE YOU AGAIN. WHAT DO YOU THINK IF I INVITE REED'S MOTHER TOO? SHE'S IN AKRON ON BUSINESS. SHE MIGHT BE ABLE TO DRIVE DOWN.

Thom replied, THAT WOULD BE GREAT. I'D BE HONORED TO MEET CAPTAIN BRANDT'S MOTHER.

ALL RIGHT. I'LL TEXT BETSY AND SEE IF IT WILL WORK FOR HER. 10:00?

PERFECT, Thom texted back. SEE YOU THEN.

She texted Betsy, who responded immediately that she would be at the café the next morning. Debbie had called her the night before and through her tears—and Betsy's—had told her about Reed's bravery and sacrifice. Debbie smiled at the thought of meeting Thom's wife and daughter with Betsy at her side. She'd have to think of a gift for Madeline. Something small but meaningful.

Next Debbie checked the voice mail. It was from Officer Jones. She pressed play.

"Hello, Ms. Albright. This is Officer Rick Jones of the Guernsey Police. I came across one piece of information about Oliver Godfrey. As a seventeen-year-old, he stopped an attack on a disabled man in St. Peter Port and held the attacker until police arrived. That's all I can find. Please call me back if you have any questions. Best wishes."

Oliver Godfrey wasn't turning out to be the deviant she had feared. It seemed she could trust her instincts—and her parents'—after all.

CHAPTER TWENTY

Saturday morning, before the café opened, Debbie and Janet had a cup of coffee together and chatted about the case.

"Where in the world could Oliver Godfrey be?" Debbie asked.

Janet took a sip of coffee and then said, "I have no idea."

"Do your parents remember any other details? Maybe the name of the person he was going to see?"

"If only."

Paulette came in at nine. The breakfast rush slowed by ten, when Thom showed up with his wife and daughter.

Debbie greeted the family, and Thom made introductions.

"Pleased to meet you." Debbie shook both of their hands, but Elena pulled her in for a hug.

"I've thought so much about you through the years," Elena said. "When Thom told me he'd met you, I asked if we could too."

"I'm so glad you did." Debbie motioned to a table in the back. "We can sit there. Betsy will join us soon. Ah, there she is now."

Betsy smiled and waved, showing off a sparkling engagement ring. She wore her silver hair short with a clip on one side, a short-sleeved dress, and dressy sandals. Every time Debbie saw her, she looked younger, healthier, and happier. Retiring to Florida had been good for both her body and spirit.

"Thom," she gushed as she stepped toward him. Reed had taken after Betsy when it came to his outgoing personality. "I'm so pleased to meet you."

After introducing everyone to each other, Debbie grabbed coffee for the adults and orange juice for Madeline. Once everyone decided what they wanted, she took their orders and gave them to Janet in the kitchen.

Janet wiped her hands on her apron and said, "I'll come out and say hello."

As Janet followed Debbie into the dining area, Betsy stood. "Janet! So good to see you."

The two hugged, and after chatting a minute, Janet said, "I'll get back to the kitchen and fix your food. I just wanted to say hi." She gave Betsy another hug then hustled away.

They started with general conversation about what had brought Thom to Ohio and why Elena and Madeline had joined him. Besides wanting to meet Debbie, they missed Thom too much to stay away. However, they were only staying a few days.

Betsy explained that she was selling her last rental property in Akron. "I'll no longer have any business ties in Ohio," she said. She patted Debbie's hand. "But I still have personal ones."

Debbie smiled, glad she felt that way.

Betsy mentioned her fiancé and that he had grandchildren. "They call me Granny Betsy."

Debbie had always believed that Betsy would be a wonderful grandmother. She was so thankful that losing Reed hadn't erased the possibility of her getting to fill that role.

When Janet called out that the order was ready, Debbie served everyone and then grabbed a scone for herself, along with the coffeepot to refill the mugs on the table.

As everyone ate, Betsy said, "Thom and Elena, it means so much to me that you gave your daughter Reed's name."

"I wish I'd told you when she was born," Thom said.

Betsy smiled. "It worked for you to tell Debbie now. And for all of us to be together. That's what matters." She wrapped both hands around her mug. "I'm thrilled that Reed's name will live on."

"Speaking of Reed," Debbie said as she pulled the Joan of Arc medallion out of her apron pocket, "this belonged to him. Madeline, your father kept it for me and then gave it to me earlier this week." She held the medallion so Madeline could see it. "The man you were named for had a great appreciation for Joan of Arc because of her faith, courage, and leadership. I'd like for you to have this, in memory of Reed, but also because faith will keep you close to God, courage will keep you on the right path, and leading will share your gifts with others."

Madeline glanced at Thom, who nodded. She accepted the medallion and murmured, "Thank you."

"You're welcome."

The adults exchanged smiles as the girl studied the medallion, and Betsy wiped away a tear.

Half an hour later, Debbie walked Thom, Elena, Madeline, and Betsy out to the parking lot and said her goodbyes. As she started back to the depot, her phone buzzed with a call from Janet.

"I'm on my way," Debbie said as she answered it.

"Good," Janet said, "because you'll never guess who's here."

"Who?"

"Oliver Godfrey."

As she stepped through the door, she saw Oliver sitting at the counter with a cup of tea and a piece of shortbread.

He slid off the stool as she approached. "I'm so sorry to have worried you," he said. "Janet told me you had no idea where I'd gone. I left a voice mail for Cindy, the proprietor of the inn where I stayed. She ran the credit card I'd left on file, so I assumed she had gotten my message."

"She said you left a note with the key."

"Well, I did." He scratched the back of his head. "But I left a voice mail first."

"Her young grandson was there when I stopped by that day looking for you," Debbie explained. "I wonder if he was the one who listened to the messages, or if there was some other mix-up. It sounded as if he hadn't followed other instructions Cindy had given him."

Oliver appeared chagrined. "I still feel bad. I asked if she would call you and let you know I was headed to Minnesota so you could let Ray know. I left my cell number in the message to give to you too. I feel horrible that he thought I let him down."

"He was eager to speak with you, but I'm sure he hasn't held it against you. How long are you staying?"

"A few days. I have a reservation at the same bed and breakfast but came here first when I hadn't heard back from you." Oliver held on to his mug of tea. "I don't know why I didn't think to call you here at the café the day I left. Blame it on jet lag or my excitement to have found my sister. I really am sorry."

"Your sister? She lives in Minnesota?"

"Yes. My baby sister. I hadn't seen her since our mum passed away twenty years ago." His eyes shone as he took a sip of tea.

"How wonderful that you saw her," Debbie said. "Honestly, I'm thankful that you're okay. My parents mentioned that you were wanting to go to Minnesota, but they didn't say it was your sister you were hoping to see."

He put down the cup as Janet approached the table. "I did mention Minnesota to them, but it's been painful not having contact with my sister for so long. And a little embarrassing. I didn't even have a phone number for her. Nothing but her email. But all of that has been remedied now. She's in a good place, much better than the last time I saw her. She was terribly hurt by our mother's death. She got married, moved to America, and kind of dropped out of sight for a while."

Debbie glanced at Janet. "Did you tell Oliver about Ray's jacket?"

"No," Janet replied.

"What happened?" Oliver asked at the same time.

"It's been missing since the morning after the ceremony," Debbie answered as Ian came through the front door.

"Hello, Oliver." Ian strode toward the trio, his hand outstretched. "Janet told me you were here." Oliver stood, and the two shook hands. "It's good to see you."

"Likewise," Oliver said. "I'm sorry I've caused all of you such worry. I just heard about Ray's jacket. I doubt it looked very good on my part to go missing the morning the jacket disappeared."

"I wouldn't say that, but I have needed to talk to you," Ian told him.

"Certainly. As I just told Debbie and Janet, I left a message for the innkeeper where I was staying, asking her to contact Debbie for me. But it appears she didn't get the message." Oliver took out his phone. "You might not think this is necessary, but I want to confirm I was in Minnesota. I have time-stamped photos of myself with my sister and nephew at the Mall of America."

"I would like to see those," Ian confirmed.

Oliver tapped his phone and showed them photos of himself with a woman who appeared to be in her forties and a young man who was probably in his early twenties. "I drove through the night. Allison and her son and I were at the mall on Friday afternoon, after I took a nap at my sister's house." He tapped the photo of them by the official Mall of America sign to reveal the time stamp.

"This is very helpful, Oliver," Ian said.

Oliver went on. "I hadn't met my nephew before. His father is American, which is why they moved to the States." He swiped his phone. "These photos are even better. I was on the road by eight the evening of the ceremony after my sister messaged me. I stopped for coffee in New Philadelphia and took some photos there." He held up his phone. "I really like the log cabins in the park." He swiped again. "And these grain elevators. I don't know that I've ever seen any this big."

Ian smiled. "Thank you, Oliver. I have one more question for you."

"What would that be?" Oliver asked.

"What size shoe do you wear?"

Oliver held up his foot, shod in a brown boot. "In the UK, six. In Europe, thirty-nine. Let's see. I tried on a pair of shoes in Minneapolis. I think they were a seven. Why do you ask?"

"We may have a shoe print from whoever took the jacket. It's a size ten."

Oliver smiled. "Then I'm really off the hook."

Ian clapped him on the shoulder. "You sure are."

Relieved, Debbie said, "I know Ray would love to talk with you when you're able."

"I could stop by after I check back into the bed and breakfast," Oliver said. "Would you be so kind as to give him a call for me? I don't want to startle him. And is there a chance you could join us, Debbie?"

"I'd love to." Debbie glanced around the café. There weren't many customers left. "I'll call Ray right now. How about I meet you at Good Shepherd? Does three thirty sound okay? That'll give me time to close the café and clean up."

"Perfect." He gave her a broad smile, his hazel eyes bright. "I can have lunch here before I go check in."

Ian left, and Oliver polished off a chicken club sandwich and headed to the B and B.

Janet asked, "What else can I do to help prove Ray was the one who rescued Adele? Is there someone overseas who could corroborate his story?"

Debbie's eyebrows shot up. "Someone living?"

Janet gave her a funny look. "Well, yes, preferably."

"There were three young women Ray might have written to about the rescue. Alié and Anne Dumas, and an Edith whose last name I don't know. Anne's health was poor, so I doubt there's any chance she's alive. Frankly, I doubt Edith and Alié are either. They'd be Ray's age or older."

"What if they told one of their children about Ray, like Oliver's mother told him?"

"Maybe."

"When you see Ray tonight, will you ask him for their full names and their last known locations?"

"You bet," Debbie said. "Thanks, Janet. You're the best."

When she arrived at Good Shepherd at 3:25, Ray and Oliver were sitting in the front lobby.

"Debbie!" Oliver called out. "Come join us."

Each had a cup of tea, and a box of Janet's shortbread sat between them. Oliver had purchased it before he left the café.

"There's tea in the dining hall if you'd like a cup," Ray said to Debbie.

She got one and then joined the two men. "Is it all right if I interrupt the two of you for a quick moment and ask Ray a couple of questions?"

"Be my guest," Oliver said.

"What do you need?" Ray asked.

"Edith's last name—a married name if you have it. And the last location you had for her. Same with Alié and Anne."

Ray crossed his arms and mulled it over. "Edith married a man named Alec Marshall sometime in the late forties. He was a doctor she'd worked with after the war. They settled in Hastings. The last time I corresponded with her was probably in the midsixties."

Debbie started a text to Janet with the information. "What about the Dumas sisters?"

"Alié and Anne both stayed in Paris. Alié was single until sometime in the fifties. She married a journalist named Marc Bernard, which made sense because she was a journalist too. Anne lived with them until her death about ten years later."

"Did Edith or Alié have children?"

"Both of them did," Ray said. "Alié had one, a girl. And Edith had five boys."

"So you wrote to them for at least twenty years after the war?"

"I did."

"How about Leland Clark? Did he continue to write to them too?"

"He didn't," Ray said. "I think they said the last time they heard from him was four or five years after the war ended."

"Interesting," Debbie said, updating her text. "I'm texting Janet about all of this, by the way. She was wondering if either Edith or Alié might have told their children about you rescuing Adele."

"I never told Edith or Alié."

"Why not?"

"We didn't talk about that sort of thing back then. Once the war was over, we all wanted to move on." Ray took a sip of his tea. "But, come to think of it, Edith found out somehow, because she mentioned it in a letter."

"How do you think she found out?"

"It must have been from Sergeant Clark," Ray answered. "I don't know how else she would have known."

"Do you still have Edith's letters?"

He shook his head. "I kept them in a box in the basement. Sadly, they were ruined when a pipe broke."

"I'm sorry. What a loss."

Ray shrugged. "I can't take any of it with me. But I was grateful that I kept the letters from Eleanor, my parents, and Gayle in the attic."

Debbie smiled at him. "Maybe Janet can track down someone who heard your story."

"Maybe." Ray smiled back. "But don't count on it. It's no loss to me if Heather Clark thinks I stole her father's story. I know what happened. Perhaps I won't remember in time, but for now I remember my story."

CHAPTER TWENTY-ONE

As Adele reached the mine, Ray lunged forward, his hands outstretched. He pushed her as hard as he could just before her foot landed.

Ray had barely hit the ground before he threw himself on top of Adele, determined to protect her if the device detonated. An explosion sent him and Adele both flying. It wasn't a full blast, like the one that injured the engineer, but pain seared through his knee, and he knew he'd been hit.

He rolled off Adele and onto his side, grabbing at his knee and groaning.

Adele scrambled to him, tears streaming down her face. "I'm so sorry. I didn't see you. I was in a hurry. Are you all right?"

"I'm alive," Ray managed to gasp out. "So are you. That's what matters." He looked her over. "Are you hurt at all?"

"Not much," she said. "Just my hands hurt where they scraped the dirt."

Sergeant Clark yelled from the fence, "What happened?"

Adele looked at Ray. "What did happen?"

"The mine exploded. Not with as much force as I was afraid it would." He gritted his teeth to keep from moaning. "Stay beside me in case there's another mine around." The grass in the field had grown knee-high. There could be other mines the engineers hadn't found.

"I thought they were done with this field," Adele said.

"Not quite." Ray gasped in pain.

"Zink!" Sergeant Clark bellowed. "What's going on?"

Ray turned his head toward the fence and spoke as loudly as he could. "The mine detonated. I'm not sure if it went off all the way or if there could be others. Adele and I are going to stay right here. I'm injured."

"I'll get the engineers and a medic," Sergeant Clark yelled back. "Hold tight."

"You're bleeding," Adele said.

Ray managed to pull the tourniquet he carried out of his pocket. "Can you help me?"

"I'll try."

He handed Adele the tubing. *"I need you to twist this around my thigh and tie it in a knot."*

"I can do that."

Ray hoped the blood wouldn't be too disturbing for her. Because of the amount, he couldn't tell where all he was injured.

"We'll have to put it over my pants." He pointed to the spot. "Wrap it around here, and then pull it really tight."

As she worked, he said, *"I'm sorry you're not down at the dock."*

"You shouldn't be sorry. It's my fault this happened to you."

"It is not," he answered firmly, thinking of the Nazis who had ordered the invasion of Guernsey, the ones who had ordered the mines to be planted, and the German engineers who planted them. All the way up the command chain to Hitler himself. "Don't ever think this is your fault."

She sniffled as someone shouted.

"They're here," Adele said through her tears.

As the engineers neared them, followed by the medic, Adele said, *"He saved my life. Please save his."*

Another medic arrived with a stretcher. One of the engineers led Adele out of the field while four men carried Ray on the stretcher.

"We think that was the last mine in the field," one of the engineers said. "At least we hope it was."

Ray couldn't imagine how long the citizens of Guernsey would have to live with the threats of hidden mines. As they reached the fence, a man came up the road, dressed in a British uniform.

"Dad!" Adele sprinted toward him and hurled herself into his arms.

The man was gaunt, but he laughed as he lifted his daughter. "Adele!"

Tears flooded Ray's eyes and ran down his temples. Sergeant Clark stepped to his side.

The medic said, "I know your pain is bad. Hold on. I'll give you a shot of morphine."

Ray winced. "The pain isn't why I'm crying. She came so close to not being here, to missing seeing her dad by mere moments."

The medic patted Ray's arm. "A truck is on the way. We'll get you on the next boat out."

Ray hoped he'd be sent back to Wraxall, but the 74th General Hospital was in the process of closing. He arrived at the Netley Hospital near Southampton sometime in the night. During surgery, the doctors set his broken kneecap and cleaned shrapnel out of his knee and thigh. For better or for worse, it was the same leg that had been shot the previous fall.

The doctor said he'd hoped he could keep his leg. "Although if it's of no use, keeping it won't do you any good."

Ray wrote letters to Edith, Alié, and Anne, saying he'd been injured by a mine on Guernsey but not giving any more details than that. All wrote back immediately. Anne sent a bookmark. Edith sent a page of jokes she'd heard from American soldiers. Alié sent sheet music to "Le Chant Des Partisans," the number one song in France. She said they could sing it together the next time they saw each other.

Ray wrote her back saying his French hadn't improved but he would be happy to play for her to sing.

After four weeks, a doctor removed the cast. Several of the wounds hadn't healed, and Ray returned to surgery. Even on the southern coast of England, the summer heat made the hospital uncomfortable. Ray felt cranky and restless and thought about Eleanor constantly. He daydreamed about her reappearing in Dennison when he returned.

One day he received an envelope from Sergeant Clark with a short note. Hope you're doing well, Zink.

With any luck, I'll be able to visit soon. Adele Martin gave me a letter to pass on to you.

The letter from Adele read:

Mr. Ray Zink,

My grandmother, my father, and I all want to thank you for saving my life. I hope you are recovering and that your leg is doing fine. I will never forget you.

Sincerely,

Adele Martin

Ray quickly responded to both letters, intending to get them in the post the next day.

But that afternoon, Sergeant Clark showed up in Ray's room with a weak, "Surprise."

Clark seemed stressed again and on edge. Another Royal Engineer had been injured dismantling a mine, and a civilian had been killed on a beach on the other side of the island.

Clark was headed to Wraxall to tell Edith goodbye before going on to Liverpool. "I'm headed home," he said to Ray. "Any chance you're ready to go too?"

Ray wished he was. "No. I have an infection that isn't clearing up. The ship ride home is too much of a risk right now."

"I'm sorry to hear that," Sergeant Clark said. "I was hoping we could end our service together."

The only thing Ray would have liked more than going home was a letter from Eleanor letting him know where she was and that she was all right. "Hopefully, I'll be able to leave in a few weeks."

Sergeant Clark couldn't stay long. He had a train to catch. "I'll tell Edith I saw you."

Ray gave Sergeant Clark the letter he'd written to him. "I have a letter for Adele too."

"I'll send it to her," Sergeant Clark said. "I can mail it at the train depot."

"Thank you." Ray added his Dennison address to the letter and then put it in an envelope. He reached for the coins on the table by his bed.

Sergeant Clark said, "I'll pay for the postage."

Ray hoped Adele would write him back. Perhaps she and Gayle would like to become pen pals. Or perhaps she would send him updates through the years about her grandmother, her father, and herself. He'd like to know that she was all right. He didn't hold out much hope for her mother, and he didn't know about her brothers, but maybe they still had a chance of returning home.

Before he told Sergeant Clark goodbye, he asked, "Should I write to you at your home address, or will you be back in college by the fall semester?"

"I hope to be in school. I wrote a letter asking to be readmitted. But write to me at my home address, since I don't know where I'll be living. My mother will forward the letter to me wherever I land."

"Will do," Ray said. "Make sure you write me back."

"I will," Sergeant Clark said. "We'll see each other soon. Maybe you can come visit once I make it to Harvard."

Ray smiled. "I've never been to Boston. I'd like that." As Sergeant Clark turned toward the door, Ray said, "Don't tell Edith about me pushing Adele out of the way, all right? I did what anyone else would have done."

A pained expression passed over Sergeant Clark's face. "I won't say a word."

It wasn't until September, weeks after the Japanese surrendered, that Ray was finally released to travel home. He sailed out of Southampton.

When he arrived at the Dennison Depot, Eileen stood on the platform as if she was waiting for someone. As he wobbled off the train on his crutches, she called out, "Ray, I heard you might be on this train." She stepped forward to take his backpack. A second *later his father and mother and Gayle rushed out of the depot onto the platform too.*

They all hugged and laughed and cried. Ray peered over their shoulders a couple of times, hoping to see Eleanor. But she didn't appear.

The next day, he walked back to the depot and found Eileen. "Any word of Eleanor?" he asked.

She shook her head. "I'm sorry."

Ray wouldn't give up hope. His first concern was Eleanor's safety. Something must have happened. The Eleanor he knew wouldn't simply disappear without a word.

It took a couple more months of rest and good food, but finally Ray was able to walk with a cane and then unassisted. The parks department hired him as a landscaper, which was the perfect activity to bring him more healing. Working outdoors, creating beauty, and taking care of plants soothed his soul. It gave him plenty of time to thank the Lord for each day and to pour out his grief over Eleanor and all he'd experienced during the war. Eventually, he was able to leave Eleanor with the Lord.

He moved back into his childhood home after his parents passed, and tended his mother's roses and his own forget-me-nots. Life was good. Being home wasn't what he expected without Eleanor, but he was happy *and had no complaints. Every single day was a gift, and his job with the parks department turned into a career. God gave him a good life.*

And now he was near the end of it. Ninety-eight years young. Just last year, thanks to Debbie, he'd found out that Eleanor had come down with polio after she left Dennison for what she'd planned to be a short time. But fate had intervened, and she had never returned. Eventually she'd married a disabled World War II vet. Both Ray and Eleanor had led good, long lives. Just not together.

He often thought of the song "Down Forget-Me-Not Lane" that Alié had sung so beautifully. They'd all survived the rain. Life hadn't been perfect, but compared to the war, they'd lived under the rainbow on Forget-Me-Not Lane ever since. Ray never considered himself as anything special. He merely did his duty. He would always remember the men he'd served with. Those who survived—and those who didn't.

And the people along the way. The war was a horrible experience, but the people he'd come to care for? They were who he remembered.

Now, he guessed, he was the last one left.

CHAPTER TWENTY-TWO

On Monday morning when Debbie arrived at the café, Janet was smiling from ear to ear. "I have good news."

"You do?"

"Yes. I got an email from London this morning."

Debbie froze. "From Edith?"

Janet grimaced. "Not that good, I'm afraid. Edith passed away over twenty years ago. But I heard from her son. He's a doctor in Chelsea."

"What did he say?"

Janet picked up a piece of paper from the counter. "I printed out his response. He posted some of the memories of the war that his mother wrote down for her sons when she was in her fifties."

"Oh, wow." Debbie read quickly.

Leland Clark came to visit me one last time in Wraxall before he shipped out to the US. He told me that our friend Ray Clark saved the life of a ten-year-old girl on Guernsey when he valiantly dove and shoved her out of the way before she stepped on a mine. Ray's leg fell on the mine as he saved her, partially detonating the charge and badly wounding his leg. Thankfully, he didn't lose it. I corresponded with Ray for several years after the war, but he never mentioned saving the girl. I don't know if it was out of humility or the desire not to relive the worst of the war. I suspect a little of both.

Debbie hugged Janet. "This is exactly what we need. How did you get in touch with him?"

"Alec, her oldest son, has a website with photos of his parents from the war. I found it by searching for 'Edith Burns Marshall.' I contacted him through the website."

"Nice." Debbie hugged Janet again. "Thank you."

Oliver stopped by the Whistle Stop for breakfast before driving to Pittsburgh to catch his flight to London the next day. After he ordered tea and a strawberry scone, he said, "I really enjoyed talking with Ray on Saturday and hearing more of his story. I'd love to stay up to date on how he's doing. And would you let me know when the jacket turns up?"

"Yes to both. What works best? Texts? A messaging app?" Debbie tapped her phone. "Good old-fashioned emails?"

He laughed and gave her his phone number and email address, which she added to her contacts. "Thanks. I'll be sure to keep you posted. Do you remember if your mother ever got a letter from Ray?"

Oliver shook his head. "I think she would have mentioned if they'd corresponded. She always spoke so highly of him. We all knew she owed her life to Ray Zink, which meant we did too. I found other letters after she passed—from her father during the war and from me once I left the island, that sort of thing. I would have taken note of a letter from Ray Zink."

"That's what I thought," Debbie said. "I have one more question, if that's all right."

Oliver gave her an encouraging smile.

"Did your mother talk about her mother or about an uncle who operated an illegal radio on Guernsey during the war? Ray remembers that both were captured by the Germans."

Oliver nodded. "They were. But miraculously, they survived. My grandmother had typhus but was freed from the concentration camp in time for it to be treated. My great-uncle was literally in line for the gas chamber when his camp was liberated by Allied forces."

Debbie gaped at him. "Wow."

"It was unbelievable," Oliver agreed. "They were both haunted by what they experienced for the rest of their lives, but they were a big part of my childhood. I consider myself lucky. So many of my friends grew up with families that had gaping holes because of relatives lost in the war. It almost seemed unfair that my family was intact."

"A form of survivor's guilt," Debbie murmured.

"There was a lot of heartache on the island after the Germans left." He smiled sadly. "My grandparents, my great-uncle, and my great-grandmother lived near us and actively worked to heal that heartache. They made my childhood absolutely idyllic. If every child was loved as much as I was growing up, the world would be a better place."

Eventually, they said their goodbyes and Oliver left as Patricia, Harry, and Crosby arrived. "Any word on Ray's jacket?" Patricia asked.

"No," Debbie answered as her phone buzzed with a text from Greg.

I SWUNG BY THE HOUSE FOR SOME PAPERWORK AND THE MAIL HAD BEEN DELIVERED ALREADY. I GOT THE MORNING REPORTS!

THANK YOU FOR HELPING ME. COULD I COME BY THIS AFTERNOON AND TELL YOU WHAT THEY SAY? I'LL ASK MOM TO STAY SO I CAN TELL HER TOO. I CAN BE THERE RIGHT AFTER YOU CLOSE IF THAT WORKS FOR YOU. YOU MIGHT WANT TO DASH HOME WHEN YOU GET A CHANCE AND SEE IF THE ONES YOU ORDERED ARRIVED TOO.

Debbie texted back, THANKS FOR LETTING ME KNOW. THIS AFTERNOON WORKS FINE FOR GETTING TOGETHER. I'LL CHECK MY MAIL ASAP.

She put in Harry's and Patricia's orders and then asked Janet if it was all right if she ran home for a minute, explaining why.

Janet's eyes lit up. "You'd better, if only because I need to know too."

Ten minutes later Debbie was out of breath and back at the café with the packet of morning reports.

"What did you find out?" Janet asked.

"I haven't opened them yet," Debbie said.

Janet glanced around the café. "It's slow right now. Or do you want to wait for Ray?"

"Not necessarily. He gave me permission to order them and read them. He said he wouldn't be surprised by anything in the reports. He lived it. He remembers."

"What do you have there?" Harry asked.

Debbie held up the envelope. "The morning reports from specific days during Ray's time of service during World War II."

"Goodness," Harry said. "You have history in your hand."

"I do indeed." A lump formed in Debbie's throat. She opened the packet and took out the documents from mid-September 1944. She skimmed the weather, number of troops, and position of the enemy. Next was the list of injuries. She scanned through the information and then said, "Here it is. 'Specialist Ray Zink was hit in the leg by enemy fire on the banks of the Geul after he pulled Sergeant Leland Clark from the river. Sergeant Clark shot himself in the leg as he walked into the river, prior to being rescued by Specialist Zink.'"

"Yikes," Janet said.

"So this is information Ray didn't know?" Harry asked.

"That's right," Debbie answered.

"Could Ray have forgotten?" Patricia asked. "If he didn't realize it when it happened, it seemed someone would have let him know."

"He never went back to that unit," Debbie explained. "After recovering from their injuries, Ray and Leland were assigned to work with Royal Engineers clearing mines in England."

"So what does Ray believe happened?" Patricia asked.

"Ray believes that Leland was shot by a German soldier from across the river." Debbie regretted reading the information out loud. She would have told Ray first before sharing it with others if she'd known the information was so startling. Leland Clark had shot himself, possibly to get away from the front, based on what Ray had said about his state of mind.

"What are you going to do with the information?" Janet asked.

"You know what I want to do?"

Janet folded her arms. "I can imagine. Send a copy to Heather Clark?"

"Exactly," Debbie said.

Patricia pushed her chair back. "Hold on. Don't do anything rash. Do you think this will be new information to Heather Clark too?"

"Yes. She believes her father was never awarded the Purple Heart he deserved. She's thinking about petitioning for one."

Patricia's eyebrows shot up. "Well, someone would check the morning reports, and she'd find out then."

"Which would explain why Leland Clark never pursued a Purple Heart," Harry said. "He knew someone would check the morning reports. Whether he shot himself intentionally or not, he knew he didn't qualify because the wound hadn't been delivered by an enemy."

"Exactly," Patricia said. "Would you like my opinion?"

"Certainly," Debbie said.

"Don't say anything to Heather yet. First give Ray the information and see what he wants to do. I get it that Heather has been obnoxious about all of this, but—"

"I'll say," Debbie said. "And we haven't told you the half of it." She explained how Heather accused Ray of stealing her father's story of saving Adele Martin, a story Leland told as early as the midsixties. But Oliver Godfrey had been told since he was a boy that it was Ray Zink who had saved his mother's life.

"Oh no," Patricia said. "It sounds like a story of stolen valor told by a man desperate for a way to redeem himself. I'm guessing telling Heather all of this will rock her world."

"Doesn't she deserve to know the truth?" Debbie demanded.

Patricia gave Debbie a sympathetic smile. "I understand how you would feel that way, but I don't think it's your place to make that decision," she said. "You need to talk with Ray and see what he wants. It's his story and his reputation. Heather isn't intentionally trying to mislead anyone. She believes what her father said and therefore believes she's protecting his legacy. Imagine being told that your father wasn't the good, courageous man you have always believed him to be. Her memory of him will be poisoned. I don't think that's what you want to happen, not when you stop and think about it."

Debbie took a deep breath. "You're right. Thanks for slowing me down. I'll visit with Ray later this afternoon."

A few minutes after Debbie flipped the sign to Closed and Paulette wiped the last table, Greg opened the door, carrying a manila envelope. "How are my two favorite ladies doing?"

"Curious." Paulette smiled at her son.

"Me too." Debbie motioned to a table. "Have a seat. Want a cup of coffee?"

"No thank you. I've reached my limit for the day." As they sat down, Greg asked, "Did you get Ray's morning reports?"

"Yes," Debbie said.

"And?"

She told him about Leland Clark's self-inflicted wound.

"Wow. That isn't a good look for someone who claimed someone else's story of heroism, is it?"

"Not at all," Debbie agreed. "I'll go by Good Shepherd and talk to Ray about it after I finish here. What did you find out?"

Greg beamed. "My grandfather was a hero. His squad came under a surprise nighttime attack by the Germans after the private on guard fell asleep." Greg opened the envelope, pulled out a sheet of paper, and began to read. "'Sergeant Connor, who wasn't on guard duty, selflessly defended their position by rushing the attackers, wounding three of them, and giving the other members of the squad time to take cover in the trees. Unfortunately, Sergeant Connor was hit by enemy fire and killed.'" Greg glanced up. "The guard who fell asleep was killed too, an eighteen-year-old from New Mexico. Grandpa Ted is listed with the survivors."

Paulette reached out and took Greg's hand. "I'm glad you have the information now. Does it help?"

"Yes. It feels like the closure we've been missing for so long," he said. "Grandpa Ted and Grandma would have known all this, but I can't fault them for not talking about it. Both must have held life-long grief over Grandpa Earl's death."

Paulette nodded. "And your dad too."

"Do you know what happened to Grandma's Bible?" Greg asked.

Paulette shook her head. "One of your aunts probably has it."

"It was her faith that got her through, don't you think?"

"Definitely," Paulette replied. "And the love between her and her kids and Grandpa Ted. Remember, just because they didn't talk about Earl Sr. in front of us doesn't mean they forgot him. I imagine the older kids and Vivian and Ted remembered him every day. As we do when it comes to those we've loved."

"What a comfort they must have been to each other," Greg said thoughtfully.

Paulette glanced from Greg to Debbie. "I know they were."

An hour later, as she sat in the lobby of Good Shepherd with Ray, Debbie watched his face as he read the morning report. When he finished, he took off his reading glasses and said, "Well that's a surprise. I knew he'd been shot, but like I told you before, I thought the bullet came from a German soldier across the river."

"Did you ever suspect that he shot himself?"

"No. I never would have expected that out of Sergeant Clark." Ray took a deep breath. "He must have held his leg up as he shot. But still, the angle would have been off. I'm guessing Hollingsworth figured out it was self-inflicted. That's why he said I'd be getting a Purple Heart and didn't mention Sergeant Clark."

"Could it be a mistake that it was a self-inflicted wound?"

"I don't think so. It would also explain why Sergeant Clark never sought a Purple Heart. He knew he wouldn't be awarded one."

"Do you think we should tell Heather?"

"I should talk to her," Ray said. "I want her to know that this doesn't speak less of her dad. He was under immense pressure. Everyone handles it differently. I can certainly understand being desperate to leave the front and go home. I don't want this to get out. I don't want a deceased Leland Clark judged by his breaking point at such a young age."

"I've already told a few people—Janet, Patricia, Harry, Greg, and Paulette," Debbie confessed. "They were there when I first read the report."

"Just let them know not to tell anyone else," Ray advised, patting her hand. "Don't worry. They can be trusted."

"Patricia would agree with you about not telling others. I'm beginning to understand that too. I got so caught up in my search for the truth that I didn't think about how devastating it might be to an entire family."

"Would you contact Heather and see if we can take her out to lunch?" Ray handed the document back to Debbie. "We can give her the morning report so she can read exactly what happened."

"Absolutely." Debbie took out her phone. "I'll call her right now." As she tapped on Heather's phone number, she said, "I'll probably have to leave a message."

But Heather answered the call immediately. "Hi, Debbie. Have you found the jacket?"

"No. But I'm at Good Shepherd with Ray. We're wondering if we could come to Columbus and take you out to lunch sometime soon."

"How nice. Is this some sort of truce?" She laughed. "I'm kidding. I'd love that. And I just had a lunch cancellation for tomorrow. Would you care to meet me at the Capitol Diner around noon?"

"Perfect," Debbie said. "See you then."

The next morning, after the breakfast rush, Debbie had a text from Greg. WOULD YOU LIKE TO GO TO DINNER TONIGHT? A NICE RESTAURANT. THE BOYS ARE HAVING DINNER AND A MOVIE NIGHT WITH MY MOM. I CAN PICK YOU UP AT 7.

SOUNDS GREAT, Debbie texted back. SEE YOU THEN.

Debbie left the café a few minutes later to pick Ray up for their trip to Columbus. Paulette was happy to work all day and help Janet close the café.

On the way, the topic of conversation landed on Ray's missing jacket and who might have taken it. "Who have you ruled out?" Ray asked.

"Definitely Oliver," Debbie answered. "His alibi is solid. He left town before the jacket went missing, right after he arrived back at the bed and breakfast after leaving Good Shepherd that night."

"And Carl's been cleared?"

"Yes," Debbie said. "And Elwood. And Jonathon Bell has been cleared too."

"So who does that leave?"

"Heather."

Ray wiped his hands on his slacks. "But why would she risk her career to steal my jacket?"

"Her father risked his career to steal your story."

"Not really," Ray said. "His chances of being caught fabricating a story were a lot less back then." He glanced out the window. "Besides, isn't Heather in her forties? Do you think she could shimmy through that window?"

"She's in good shape," Debbie said. "But perhaps someone crawled through the window for her."

Ray hesitated a moment and then asked, "But who would do that? I can't see Ruby doing it."

"Neither can I. What did she say about Graham that evening when we all had dinner at Good Shepherd? Something about his already having plans in Columbus."

"That probably rules him out, then," Ray said.

"If that's actually where he was, yes. But maybe Heather said that so we wouldn't suspect him, and then he didn't leave town when she claimed." Debbie thought a moment. "It's interesting that Jonathon came back to Dennison to talk with Ian about all of this, but Heather didn't. When I called her, she was offended and somewhat defensive."

"I wouldn't read too much into that," Ray said. "I've been hoping this whole time that the jacket has just been misplaced and that it will show up soon. I still can't believe someone would steal it."

"I understand that," Debbie said. "Of course, that's the best scenario for everyone, but I think if it had somehow been misplaced it would have been found by now. Or if someone took it and decided to return it, that would have happened already."

Ray stared straight ahead. "Maybe you're right."

When they reached Columbus, Debbie had to park a block away from the restaurant. When she rolled Raymond and his chair through the door of the Capitol Diner a few minutes late, Debbie scanned the room. She didn't see Heather—but she did see a red-headed young woman. *Ruby.* She was sitting with an elderly man. Perhaps Heather was running late.

"Ruby," Debbie said, as she pushed Ray's chair up to the table.

As she turned to Debbie, Ruby smiled and then stood. "Debbie. Ray. How nice to see you again." She gestured toward the man sitting at the table. "This is my great-uncle, Tim Adams."

"Timmy Adams?" Ray extended his hand. "Isabella's little brother?"

"Yes." The man, whose hair was whitish blond as if at one point in his life it had been red, appeared confused as he stood and took Ray's hand. "And who would you be?"

"Ray Zink. I met you when you were five or so."

Tim laughed as he let go of Ray's hand. "Wow. Are you sure?"

"Yes. In Cornwall. Isabella—or Izzy as we called her back then—worked for the Royal Engineers and looked after us Yanks."

"She did indeed. That's how we ended up over here."

"Yes," Ray said. "So Izzy really did marry Leland."

Tim nodded. "And you served with him?"

"I did. In England, France, Belgium, the Netherlands, Cornwall, and on Guernsey."

"Goodness," Tim said. "And where do you live now?"

"In Dennison, where I lived for the few years before I enlisted and for the many years since I returned from the war."

Debbie pushed Ray's chair up to the place setting that didn't have a chair.

Tim sat back down. "You've been this close all along? Why in the world didn't you reach out to Leland? He would have loved to have seen you."

"I believe the answer to that may be a story for another time." Ray smiled at Tim. "How young are you now? Eighty-three?"

"Eighty-four." Tim grinned. "I just had my birthday."

"I never would have dreamed I'd see Timmy Adams again."

"I was twelve when Isabella married Leland," Timmy said. "She couldn't very well leave me behind."

Ray laughed. "No, I guess not."

Debbie sat down between Ray and Ruby. "Is Heather on her way?"

"No," Tim answered. "She had something come up but sends her regards."

"That's too bad." Debbie picked up her menu, trying to hide her disappointment. "Please tell her we missed her."

"I will." Tim patted Ruby's arm. "I came along with Ruby as moral support."

Ruby blushed. "It's true. I asked him to come. Uncle Tim always encourages me to do the right thing."

Tim had a startled expression on his face. "I have no idea what you're talking about."

Debbie studied the young woman. "Ruby, do you have something to tell us?"

After hesitating for a long moment as her face reddened, Ruby replied, "Maybe."

Before Debbie could press the issue, the waiter appeared with the specials of the day. He then took their drink orders.

After the waiter left, Tim began a story about his time in Cornwall during the war, when he'd hidden in a general's jeep for a day. Debbie would have to wait for a chance to try to get Ruby to open up.

CHAPTER TWENTY-THREE

Once their food was delivered, Debbie asked Ruby about her plans for the summer, hoping that might be a segue back to her reference of doing "the right thing."

"I'm working as an intern in Aunt Heather's office," Ruby replied.

"Is Graham an intern too?" Debbie asked.

"No." Ruby picked up half of her French dip sandwich. "He was two years ago, but he's been Heather's assistant for the last year."

Tim said to Ray, "I'm a little slow putting this together, but I'm guessing you're the World War II veteran that had the ceremony in Dennison."

"Yes, that's right," Ray answered.

"I was visiting my daughter and her family in Pittsburgh at the time," Tim said. "Otherwise, I would have been there, even without having any idea we'd met before. I'm forever grateful to you Yanks for helping us save Europe and England and Asia. For helping to save all of us."

"Thank you," Ray said.

"I asked Heather several questions over the phone about the day Ray's army jacket went missing," Debbie said.

"What happened to your jacket?" Tim asked Ray.

"We don't know," Ray answered. "That's what we're trying to figure out."

Debbie kept her gaze on Ruby. "I was hoping to ask Heather more questions, but she's not here. Ruby, do you mind if I ask you about that day?"

Ruby hesitated, and then said, "All right."

"Did you and Heather see Graham later that evening?"

"No." Ruby put her sandwich down. "Graham said he was returning to Columbus before we did. He was meeting a friend to do parkour."

"Parkour?" Debbie had heard of it as some kind of sport but couldn't remember the details. "What is that?"

Ruby rolled her eyes. "I've been told that it's a lot of climbing and jumping and stuff like that. There are a couple of courses in town. Like people run up a wall, flip, and then jump off a ledge and swing from a rope. I don't know exactly. Ninja moves or something like that."

"Interesting." Debbie speared a piece of lettuce as her suspicions shifted from Ruby to Graham. "So he met his friend in Columbia to do parkour?"

"I think that was his plan. I mean, it was earlier in the day, but I don't know exactly when he left."

"Okay." Debbie glanced at Tim, who was concentrating on his fettucine alfredo then refocused on Ruby. "Did Heather talk about Ray's jacket with you, his Purple Heart, or him rescuing Adele Martin on Guernsey?"

Ruby wrinkled her nose. "I don't want to make Aunt Heather look bad, but yes to all three."

"Can you be more specific?"

She glanced at Tim again. He nodded and said to Debbie, "Heather has her moments. Whatever Ruby tells you Heather said, please take it with a grain of salt. Heather is known for her hyperbole." He nodded at Ruby again. "Go ahead."

"Aunt Heather was upset that Ray had been awarded a Purple Heart and Bronze Star and Grandpa hadn't. Plus, we don't have Grandpa's jacket and she said—" Ruby glanced at Ray. "Please don't take this too seriously, Mr. Zink. Uncle Tim is right about Aunt Heather. She can be dramatic."

"I won't," Ray said. "Please just tell us what you can."

"All right." Ruby sighed. "She said it wasn't fair that you had a jacket and no one to pass it down to while we didn't have a jacket but had descendants in our family who want it, and the medals too." She twisted her napkin in her fingers. "And she's convinced that Grandpa wouldn't have lied about rescuing Adele Martin. In fact, her entire opinion of Grandpa seems to be based on that story."

"What do you think?" Debbie asked Ruby.

"I think there's a chance that Mr. Zink rescued the girl. Why would Oliver come all this way with a wrong name? And nothing against Grandpa, but every so often he'd exaggerate or take credit for something he didn't do. Nothing big, but still. My dad noticed it too. He said that was the way Grandpa was and that it probably served him well as a politician. But Dad told me I needed to be honest, no matter what Grandpa did."

"I see," Debbie said.

Ruby sighed. "Aunt Heather is more like Grandpa. She tends to exaggerate too. And she's always trying to take me under her wing,

WHISTLE STOP CAFÉ MYSTERIES

as if I need someone to parent me. I appreciate the internship, but Dad has been a good parent. He takes good care of me."

"I'm glad to hear it," Debbie said. "Why didn't your dad come with you today?"

"He and Heather don't get along that well. That would have annoyed her."

"Why don't they get along?"

Ruby glanced at Tim. "Why do you think they don't get along?"

"They're very different people," Tim said. "Heather is more like Leland—ambitious and driven—while James takes after Isabella—more relaxed and concerned about others. Heather is three years older than James. She wasn't born until Leland and Isabella had been married for a decade or so. They were afraid they'd never have kids."

He stopped as if considering his next words, and no one hurried him.

Tim twirled some fettuccini on his fork. "Let's just say Heather was the best thing ever. Not that James wasn't too, but they poured a lot into Heather. She followed in Leland's footsteps, becoming a lawyer and going into politics. Isabella never pressured James to be anything other than what he was. He went to law school too but eventually decided to teach instead of going into practice. Isabella saw his gifts in education, but Heather was always disappointed in her brother. Leland didn't exactly pressure James, but there were times he seemed to wish James was—well, something grander."

"How sad," Debbie said. "Tim, have you lived in Columbus ever since you left England?"

"Yes," he said. "Except for college. I went to the University of Pennsylvania. Then I moved back here, and Isabella and I opened a

British import business. I closed it after she passed. I couldn't keep doing it without her. I've been retired since. I have a son who lives here, and my daughter lives in Pittsburgh. They and my grandkids, and now a great-grandbaby, keep me busy." He smiled fondly at Ruby. "And Ruby, who is like another grandchild to me."

Ruby blinked a couple of times but smiled back. The Clark-Adams clan were certainly an interesting family.

Debbie said, "Thank you for trusting us with this, Ruby. I have one more question for you. Have you seen anything new or unusual in Heather's office? A box or bag? Something a jacket could fit in?"

Ruby pursed her lips. "Do you think Aunt Heather took it?"

"No," Debbie said. "I don't think, even though she's in great shape, that she could hoist herself through the ventilation window at the dry cleaners. But I would like to rule out the possibility that someone she knows took the jacket and gave it to her." Now that Debbie knew Graham did parkour, she was most interested in him as a suspect.

Ruby squinted. "You know, there is a new garment bag in her closet. Sometimes she brings her dry cleaning to the office before she takes it home, but that bag's been there for over a week."

"What about Graham?" Debbie asked. "Do you think he would have taken it?"

Ruby's eyes grew large. "I really think he headed back here after the ceremony. What time do you think the jacket was taken?"

"Sometime after nine."

"I don't think he was still in Dennison then. And Aunt Heather and I left right after the dinner at Ray's retirement place," Ruby said. "That would mean all of us had left Dennison by the time the jacket was taken."

Debbie was trying to figure out how to ask Ruby to open the garment bag and see what was in it when Tim said, "Why don't we get dessert to go and take it back to Heather's office? I'll unzip the garment bag and see what's in it. She's used to me being nosy."

"Good idea," Ray said. "I need to show her some morning reports from September of 1944 anyway and talk about what's in them. I'd like to do that before we leave town."

Tim ordered plenty of strawberry pie to go and then picked up the tab for lunch.

"Let me split it with you," Debbie said.

"I wouldn't hear of it," he said. "I'm happy to have been able to meet Ray again, even though I don't recall the first time. And I hope we can sort out what happened to the missing jacket."

When they arrived at Heather's office, Tim led the way, Ruby carried the bag with the pie, and Debbie pushed Ray.

Tim opened the door and called out, "Heather, we're here." He waved Ruby into the office and then Debbie and Ray.

Graham was behind a desk with a surprised expression on his face. He stood. "Hi, Ruby."

"Hi," she said. "Do you remember Debbie and Ray from Dennison?"

"That's right." He stepped around the desk and shook Ray's hand.

Debbie stepped to the side of the wheelchair and glanced at Graham's shoes. They looked like a size ten, or close. They were dress shoes, as she'd expected he'd wear at work. But in the corner was a backpack with a pair of shoes beside it. Athletic shoes. The funny-looking kind that Janet had showed her.

"Hello, Graham." Tim took the bag from Ruby, held it up, and stepped forward. "We brought pie."

Graham gave him a strained smile.

"Is Heather busy?" Tim asked.

Graham replied, "I believe so."

"Would you please tell her I'm here?" Tim smiled. "I know she'll want to see her dear old uncle."

"Uncle Tim." Heather stood in the doorway. "I thought I heard your voice. What are you doing here?"

"Hello, Heather." Tim motioned toward Debbie and Ray. "I met these lovely people for lunch. Although it's not the first time Ray and I met. It turns out Ray served in Cornwall with your dad."

"Really?" Heather said. "I know they served together in Holland and on Guernsey."

"We served in many places together," Ray said. "I knew your mother too. Isabella was a lovely young woman."

Heather crossed her arms. "Why didn't you tell me you knew my mom?"

"I had no idea who your mother was," Ray said. "Until Debbie told me Leland had married Isabella Adams. I knew her as Izzy but suspected it was the same person. Tim confirmed it."

Heather glanced from Debbie to Ray to Tim. "Well, what a surprise."

Tim held the bag up. "We brought pie."

"I have a meeting in a half hour."

WHISTLE STOP CAFÉ MYSTERIES

"We'll be sure to be out of here before then." Tim motioned to the sitting area with a big coffee table in the middle. "We have plates, napkins, and little plastic forks."

"I'll make coffee," Ruby said.

"Thank you, Ruby. I'll help," Tim said. "Heather, would you please serve the pie?"

Heather didn't seem happy about it, but she followed her uncle's instructions. Debbie pushed Ray close to the table.

Soon the smell of coffee filled the room, and Tim slipped into the hallway. When he came back, his expression was as jovial as before. Debbie had no idea whether he'd checked the garment bag in the closet or not.

Heather distributed the containers of pie, and then Ruby served the coffee. As Heather sat down in one of the wingback chairs, she said, "Ray, Dad never mentioned you were in Cornwall with him. I wonder why."

"I have no idea," Ray said. "We were there from the time we recovered from our wounds in the Netherlands until we were sent to Guernsey."

"He only mentioned your time before you were both injured and your time on Guernsey."

Ray shrugged. "Perhaps he didn't have any stories from Cornwall."

"Oh, he did. He spoke often of meeting Mom and Uncle Tim." Heather chuckled. "Of what a pill Uncle Tim was."

"Indeed," Tim said.

"A cute pill," Ray added. "I've never forgotten how uplifting it was to chat with a little guy like you. We didn't often see children."

He set his coffee cup on the table beside his half-eaten pie. "Pardon me, but since we don't have much time, I need to change the subject." He turned his attention to Heather. "Debbie solved the mystery of why your father didn't receive a Purple Heart."

Heather's face brightened. "She did?"

Debbie took the morning report from her purse and handed it to Heather. "Read the top document. It explains what happened."

Heather's face fell as she read. Then she glared at them. "I don't believe this. How do I know you didn't fabricate it?"

Tim took the document from her hand and read it. "It makes perfect sense. And it's not fabricated. I saw enough of these when Izzy took me to work with her to recognize the real thing when I see it." He extended his hand to Debbie. "Let me see the rest of the packet, if you'd be so kind."

She handed it to him, and he shuffled through the remaining papers. He passed the cover letter to Heather. "Read this. It says there are eight pages, and there are." He handed the entire packet to Heather. "How in the world would Debbie know the details to fabricate this? Ray was there, and he wouldn't know all these details, especially after he was injured."

Heather's lower lip trembled, but she lifted her chin stubbornly.

Ray leaned forward in his chair. "Heather, I know this is upsetting. But this doesn't change the fact that your father was a brave man. And a good leader. He had a breaking point, as we all did."

Squeezing her eyes shut, Heather hung her head.

"But he came back from it and continued to serve, which is remarkable. He was in charge of a squad when he was only twenty-one years old. He had immense responsibilities and burdens.

I certainly don't hold this against him. We shouldn't remember someone at their breaking point. We should remember them at their best. That's what inspires the rest of us."

Heather raised her head and gave him a weak smile. "You're right. Thank you for saying that."

"It makes me think of a prayer that Eleanor Roosevelt carried with her," Ray said. "'Dear Lord, lest I keep my complacent way, I must remember somewhere out there a person died for me today. As long as there must be war, I ask and I must answer, was I worth dying for?' I think we can apply that to not only soldiers but to all service people."

"Amen," Debbie said, echoed by Tim.

"I have no doubt Leland would have risked his life for me every day of the war—except for that night in the Netherlands when he hit rock bottom." Ray's eyes grew misty. "Knowing what I know now, I still have to say that serving with him was one of the greatest honors of my life."

"Well, this doesn't mean Dad didn't save the little girl," Heather said. Her voice was low, and she sounded exhausted.

Debbie pulled the printed email from her purse and handed it to Heather. "I have information on that too. There's a website listed at the bottom of the message where Edith Burns Marshall's World War II account is posted."

"Edith Burns? Dad mentioned her. They wrote to each other for a few years. He kept her letters, along with letters from a French woman."

"Alié Dumas," Ray supplied. "She married a journalist named Marc Bernard."

"Yes," Heather said. "He saved those letters too, along with Mom's." As she read the email, her face grew more serious. She took out her phone, probably to find the website. Then she lifted her head and met Ray's gaze. "Will you contact Jonathon with this information? Alert the media and smear Dad's good name?"

"Absolutely not. I won't be telling anyone about any of this." Ray glanced around the room. "And I ask that none of you do either. I have no idea why your dad said he saved Adele Martin, but it was most likely out of some feeling of inadequacy, perhaps due to his self-inflicted wound."

Ruby gasped, and Graham, who was back behind the desk, let out a groan. It seemed the young people, who hadn't read the reports, had caught on to what had transpired almost eighty years ago.

"I don't hold any of this against Leland," Ray said. "And I don't want any of you young people to either." He looked from Graham to Heather to Ruby. "What I do want is for all of you to realize how deceit leads to more deceit. The Bible says that whoever is dishonest with little will also be dishonest with much."

No one said anything for a long moment, and then Heather let out a big sigh. "Speaking of deceit…," she said. She handed both the morning report and the email back to Debbie then stood and said to Ray, "You've inspired me to take care of something I should have done a week ago." She headed down the hall.

Tim's eyebrows shot up. Ruby stared after her aunt. Graham buried his face in his hands.

Heather returned carrying a garment bag as Graham raised his head and said, "This isn't Heather's fault. I took it."

Debbie sighed in relief at his confession.

"No." Heather started to unzip the bag. "It is my fault. I went on and on about Dad not getting a Purple Heart and what a shame it was that we didn't have any of his uniforms. I so badly wanted a jacket to frame and a Purple Heart to put in a shadow box that I couldn't stop talking about it. Graham went for a run before he left Dennison and ran through the alley behind the dry cleaners. He knew Carl had the jacket there, and he noticed the window was open. Instead of coming back to Columbus, he stayed until after dark and went through the window."

"Size ten?" Debbie asked, pointing to the shoes by the backpack. Graham nodded.

"But I put him up to it," Heather said. "I was spouting what I thought was the truth—that Dad deserved a Purple Heart, which meant we deserved to have a jacket and that Ray had stolen Dad's story. I put it in Graham's mind, and he did it because he thought it would make me happy."

"Maybe so," Ray said, leaning forward. "But Graham, I hope you've learned a lesson. It's never worth it to compromise your own morals to please someone else. I won't press charges, but I need to know you understand how your integrity is your greatest gift to yourself—and to others."

"Yes, sir," he said. "I understand that now."

"Then I'll let Jonathon know the jacket has been recovered, but I won't be disclosing any other details. However, I will tell our police chief, Ian Shaw, the entire story. I'll be clear that I don't want to press charges."

"Thank you. I'll contact Ian Shaw too and corroborate your story," Heather said as she pulled Ray's jacket from the bag. The light from the window caught his Purple Heart and shimmered across it. "Here it is. In good shape. All the medals are exactly where they should be."

"Thank you," Ray said, taking the jacket from Heather. "I'm having a birthday party on Saturday—for my ninety-ninth—at one o'clock at Good Shepherd. You're all invited. We don't have time now, but I need to tell you about the day during the war that I hit rock bottom. It was June 22, 1944." He smiled at Heather. "It was your dad who turned it around for me."

"Thank you," Heather said. "I'd love to hear that story."

Debbie leaned back in her chair. Ray's story, Thom's story about Reed, and Greg's grandfather's story had inspired her to live her life in a way that honored all of those who had given theirs for hers. She hoped she would be worthy too.

That evening, when Debbie opened the door, Greg stood on her porch wearing slacks, a button-down shirt, and dress shoes.

"Hello," he said.

"Come on in." She held the door for him. Once he was inside, she closed the door and hugged him. She caught the musky scent of aftershave as his smooth face brushed against hers.

He pulled away. "You look lovely."

"Thank you." She'd chosen to wear a drop-waist floral summer dress. She smiled up at him. "You clean up nicely too."

He winked. "Once in a blue moon. Ready to go?"

WHISTLE STOP CAFÉ MYSTERIES

"Yes. Let me grab a sweater and my purse." She opened the hallway closet.

"How did today go with Ray?"

"Really well." They stepped onto the porch, and she closed and locked the door behind them. "Much better than I expected."

On the drive to the restaurant, she explained everything that happened, ending with, "So Ray has his jacket back."

"I'm very glad to hear that."

"He doesn't want people to know the details, but he told me I could tell you," Debbie said. "And Janet, who probably already knows because we called Ian on the way home and told him to tell Janet. Heather had already called him."

"That's great it all worked out."

"Right? I'm kind of blown away and incredibly grateful."

Greg turned into the parking lot of Buona Vita.

"Wait. We're eating here?"

"Yes." Greg pulled into a parking space. "I thought it was high time we had a real date. Sit tight." He opened his door, and Debbie waited as he stepped around his pickup and opened hers.

"Thank you." Debbie got out, and they strolled into the restaurant.

They stopped at the host stand, and Greg checked in for their reservation. The host led them through the dimly lit restaurant to the last booth. A candle burned on the table beside a single red rose in a vase, something Debbie didn't remember from any other time she'd been at the restaurant.

As she sat down, Debbie asked, "Did my parents tell you about this booth?"

Greg looked around. "No. What about it?"

"It's the one my family and I use for special occasions." She smiled at him.

He smiled back. "I hope this counts as one of those. What does Ray plan to do with his jacket now that it's been returned to him?"

"He didn't think his niece, Trudy, would want it, but she does. So it'll go to her once—" Debbie's voice wavered. "Once Ray is gone."

Greg took Debbie's hand. "That will be a sad day."

Debbie nodded.

"But it's not today." Greg's hand was warm as he firmly held hers. "What you did for Ray is spectacular. You cleared his good name and provided him with information from the war that he didn't have. You also gave him the opportunity to show grace to the Clark family."

A wave of comfort swept through Debbie. "Thank you. I'm just so relieved that the truth came out, and in a respectful way."

Greg smiled at her. "And thank you for what you did to get me the information I needed too. Having that piece of history helps me understand Grandma Vivian and Grandpa Ted better and gives me a glimpse of Grandpa Earl."

"You're welcome," Debbie said. "It's been a pretty amazing couple of weeks. And a fancy date with you is the cherry on top."

He took her hand. "I couldn't have said that better myself."

"Now that we've caught up on me, how about you fill me in on what's happening with you?"

As Greg talked, Debbie leaned back in the booth, thinking about her own Forget-Me-Not Lane. Celebratory dinners at Buona Vita with Mom and Dad as she was growing up. Her last dinner with Reed. Dinners since, some for comfort and some to celebrate. And now, dinner with Greg, in the same booth.

The evening was definitely a rainbow at the end of her own lane of memories, likely one of many more to come. She could hardly wait.

Dear Reader,

Years ago, I taught a fiction-writing workshop at my kids' middle school. One of the most memorable aspects of it was the tag-team story we wrote. Each week a different student or teacher would add a chapter to a collaborative narrative. The students totally embraced the challenge and ran with the story in creative twists and turns while preserving the continuity. It got pretty wild, but it worked!

Working with other authors on the Whistle Stop Café Mysteries reminds me of that middle-school story. Not because things get wild, but because writing the novels are always a fun, welcome challenge in my writing life.

As I planned *Down Forget-Me-Not Lane*, I knew I wanted to concentrate on Ray Zink for the historical thread. My father fought in Europe during World War II, from 1944–45, as Ray did. From previous stories, I knew Ray landed on Omaha Beach in Normandy in June of 1944, ended up fighting in the Netherlands, and then served in the Channel Islands. My challenge was to figure out which US Army division fought or served in those same places. After some research I discovered the 30th Infantry Division landed on Omaha Beach and fought in the Netherlands. I met those two components of my challenge! The book *Work Horse of the Western Front* by Robert L. Hewitt helped immensely in my research.

My next task was to figure out how to get Ray to the Channel Islands by the end of the war. I soon discovered that US Army soldiers assisted British Royal Engineers in dismantling mines on the island of Guernsey, a task perfect for Ray Zink.

Of course, I thought of my father, who passed away six years ago at the age of ninety-three, as I wrote. "Spending" time with Ray, as I remembered my dad, was a blessing. As we lose our World War II veterans (may they rest in peace), writing and reading about their stories in both fiction and nonfiction becomes even more important. I'm so happy to have been able to meet the challenge and write *Down Forget-Me-Not Lane.*

Enjoy!

Leslie Gould

P.S. I must let all the history buffs know that I took creative license with the National Archives' procedure for requesting information about World War II veterans. According to their website, https://www.archives.gov/personnel-records-center/military-personnel/morning-reports-and-unit-rosters, if you are seeking information for morning reports dated before 1968, you must go to St. Louis to retrieve them. But I needed Debbie to stay in Dennison, so the National Archives gave her special treatment!

ABOUT the AUTHOR

*L*eslie Gould is a number-one bestselling and Christy-Award winning author of over forty novels. She's also won two Faith, Hope, and Love Readers' Choice Awards and has been a finalist for the Carol Award. Leslie has a bachelor's degree in history and a Master of Fine Arts degree in creative writing. In the past, she curated the Swedenburg House Museum in Ashland, Oregon, edited a magazine, and taught writing on the university level. Currently, she writes and edits full-time. She and her husband, Peter, live in Portland, Oregon, and enjoy hiking, traveling, and spending time with their adult children and two grandbabies.

TRUTH BEHIND the FICTION

I have long been fascinated by the Channel Islands, the only British territory occupied by the Germans during World War II. Four of the seven islands—Jersey, Guernsey, Alderney, and Sark—were captured because they were too vulnerable, by both land and sea, for England to defend.

Although the islands are only ten to thirty miles from France and over two hundred miles from England, they're dependent territories of the latter. However, they're not officially part of the United Kingdom. It can all be a bit confusing to those of us not used to such a system!

Before the Germans arrived, the majority of the children on the four islands were evacuated to England for their safety. The Germans mined beaches and other areas in anticipation of England attempting to take back the islands. It was a long five years for the residents of the four islands. Prisoners of war captured by the Germans in the Soviet Union and Europe were brought to the islands and forced to work as slave laborers, constructing fortifications and tunnels. The prisoners were poorly clothed and fed, but any residents of the islands caught helping the slave laborers were captured themselves and sent away from the islands to concentration camps in Europe.

The Channel Islanders were resilient, and many resisted the Germans as best they could. By the final months of the war, the residents of the Channel Islands were near starvation. Thankfully, a ship

from Portugal arrived in December of 1944 with food and other neces-
sities. The Red Cross continued to send supplies that kept the residents
from starving until the Germans surrendered in May of 1945.

After the war, the British Royal Engineers worked to dismantle
the mines the Germans had placed all around the four islands, including on Guernsey. They were assisted by American soldiers, which
allowed me to include the island in *Down Forget-Me-Not-Lane*.
Although the majority of the mines were cleared, some unidentified
ones still remain.

While I wrote *Down Forget-Me-Not Lane*, I had the privilege of
traveling to the United Kingdom and Ireland and ventured out to a
few islands off the coast of both Ireland and Scotland. Unfortunately,
I didn't have time to include a trip to the Channel Islands—Guernsey
in particular—but the next time I make it the UK, I definitely will!

FROM the HOME-FRONT KITCHEN

Janet's Strawberry Scones

Ingredients:

Scones:

2 cups flour

¼ cup sugar

1 tablespoon baking
   powder

½ tablespoon salt

6 tablespoons cold unsalted
   butter

1 cup heavy cream plus
   1 tablespoon for brushing
   the scones

1 teaspoon vanilla extract

1¼ cup chopped fresh
   strawberries

2 teaspoons brown sugar

For the white chocolate glaze:

8 ounces white chocolate
   (not chips)

1 cup heavy whipping
   cream

Directions:

Preheat oven to 400 degrees. Line a baking sheet with parchment paper.

   In a large bowl, whisk together flour, sugar, baking powder, and salt.

Using a pastry blender, cut butter into flour mixture until mixture comes together in pea-sized crumbs.

In a small bowl, whisk together 1 cup heavy cream and vanilla extract. Drizzle liquid ingredients into flour mixture and stir until dough begins to form. Be careful not to overmix. Fold in strawberries.

Transfer dough to floured surface and bring it together until it forms a ball. Pat and press dough into a 1-inch-thick circle. Use a knife to cut the dough into 8 triangles.

Place scones on prepared baking sheet and put in freezer for 15 to 20 minutes.

After removing scones from freezer, brush tops with 1 tablespoon heavy cream. Sprinkle with brown sugar. Bake 18 to 23 minutes or until scones are golden brown on bottom and around edges. Remove from oven and cool on baking sheet for 5 minutes. Transfer to wire cooling rack.

While the scones are cooling, make the glaze. Chop white chocolate into small pieces, place in a medium bowl, and set aside. Bring heavy cream to a simmer, remove from heat, and pour over white chocolate pieces. Cover the bowl with a plate and let mixture sit for 5 minutes then stir until smooth.

Let glaze cool to the point that it is still pourable but hasn't hardened. Drizzle over scones.

Read on for a sneak peek of another exciting book
in the Whistle Stop Café Mysteries *series!*

SET THE WORLD ON FIRE

BY BETH ADAMS

*T*he lunch crowd finally started to clear out. Janet Shaw stood behind the register and rang up the bill for one of the last tables. Tuesdays weren't usually this busy, and while Janet was grateful for the business, she was ready to pack it in. Paulette Connor—who helped out in the dining room most days—had already left, since they were half an hour past their normal closing time.

"I'll watch for your booth at the fair," Janet said to the departing customers, waving to them as they walked toward the door.

The older couple had told her that they were in town for the homecoming festival—officially the American Soldiers Homecoming Tribute Festival—that Kim Smith had arranged at the Dennison Railroad Depot Museum. Volunteers at the Dennison Depot had famously welcomed and fed soldiers passing through on their way to and coming home from World War II, and the little town had a reputation for honoring the soldiers who had fought for their country. Kim, who ran the museum, had arranged the event to celebrate the local veterans, as well as to attract some attention to the museum and its newly refurbished Pullman car, which could be rented out to stay in overnight.

Janet had been chatting with the couple and learned that they made military-themed T-shirts and sweatshirts, which they would sell from a booth at the festival. "I hope you sell a lot," Janet said.

"Thank you," the woman said. "We'll be looking for you."

Janet waved, and they walked out.

Her best friend and business partner, Debbie Albright, emerged from the kitchen with a bucket of soapy water in her hands.

"This bodes well for the homecoming festival," Debbie said. "It doesn't even start for a few days, and there are already so many new people in town." She dunked a dishcloth in the bucket and started to wipe down the counter.

"It's great," Janet said. "I'm so happy for Kim. It'll be really good for the museum."

"It's not going to be bad for us either," Debbie said. "As long as we can keep up."

"We'll manage fine. We always do."

Janet glanced over at the table occupied by Austin and Carrie Wilson, fellow members of Faith Community Church, and old friends. She didn't want to rush them, especially as they seemed to be in some kind of deep discussion. She would work on cleaning the rest of the dining room, and perhaps by the time she had everything else done, they'd be ready to go. She took another dishcloth and started wiping the tables and straightening chairs.

When she came to the corner table, she spotted something on the floor underneath it. Janet bent down, tugged it free, and saw it was a receipt.

New Philadelphia Military Surplus Store, it said at the top. Dated that morning. Someone had bought a glass bottle, gloves, some rope, a knife, a few T-shirts—all kinds of random things, apparently.

She tried to remember who'd been sitting at this table. Possibly that man who dealt in antique firearms. He was also here for the festival and planned to set up a booth to sell his historic weapons. Collectible Winchester repeating rifles and such, he'd told her. She didn't know if he'd need this receipt, but it must have fallen out of the black duffel bag he'd had with him. She'd keep it in case he came back for it. She folded the receipt, tucked it in her pocket, and kept cleaning the dining room.

Finally, when the Wilsons' table was the last one left to clean, Carrie raised her head and seemed to realize for the first time that they were alone.

"I'm so sorry, Janet." Carrie pushed herself up, and Austin reluctantly stood as well. "I didn't realize how late it had gotten."

"That's all right," Janet said. "Did you enjoy your meal?"

"It was delicious, as always," Austin said. He was tall and broad-shouldered, a vestige of his former career as a Marine. These days, Austin was a pediatric nurse at the hospital who sometimes played the trumpet in the community band. He was heading up a clothing drive to help needy veterans as part of the festival. He and Carrie had come in for lunch after a meeting with Kim Smith.

"I'm so glad," Janet said. "I don't want to rush you, but I can ring you up whenever you're ready."

"We're ready." Carrie finished her lemonade and set the glass on the table. "I'm sorry we took so long. We got talking and lost track of time."

"No worries whatsoever. Thank you for the project you've taken on for this weekend. It's a great cause."

"We hope it helps," Carrie said. "There are so many veterans in need."

"Ian went through his closet, so I have a bunch of clothes to donate," Janet said. Her husband had needed to clean out his closet for a while, truthfully, and this was a good excuse.

"Feel free to bring them by our place before the festival," Carrie said. "It's all coming back to our place anyway, and we'll have limited space in the car, so we may need to make several trips. If you brought your donation to us ahead of time, you'd likely save us a trip."

"No problem. I'll bring it over to you sometime this week," Janet said.

"Thank you so much." Carrie hoisted her purse onto her shoulder, and she and Austin walked to the register, where Debbie waited to ring them up. Debbie punched the buttons on the register for their meal, and Carrie grabbed a pack of Black Jack gum and a package of Necco wafers from the display of nostalgic candy they had for the festival. "We'll take these too," Carrie said. "Tyler loves this stuff."

"Better add some of that peanut candy," Austin said.

"I didn't see that. He is a fiend about it." Carrie grabbed another package and set them all on the counter.

"How is Tyler?" Janet asked as Debbie added the candy to their total.

"He's doing as well as can be expected," Carrie said. "He's struggling, but he's doing all right, I suppose."

Tyler, Carrie and Austin's son, had been a baseball star at the high school. He'd won sponsorships, had been recruited for travel teams, and even played in the High School World Series. He'd gone off to Ohio State on a baseball scholarship three years ago. But an injury early in the season his sophomore year had blown out his knee, requiring surgery, and the physical therapy had taken longer than expected. He'd eventually lost his scholarship and his sponsorship and had to come home. "He's working on getting back into shape, and we're hoping to find another school for him."

"I'll be praying for him," Janet said as Debbie swiped Austin's credit card. "I bet once he's fully recovered and playing, colleges will be fighting over him."

"I hope so, but mostly we hope he gets through this rough patch okay," Austin said.

"It can be really hard at this age," Janet said. Her own daughter, Tiffany, was just two years younger than Tyler, and though Tiffany was doing well and enjoying being home for the summer, Janet knew she had her moments. It could be so hard to find one's footing at her age. "But Tyler's a good kid. He'll get through this."

"Thank you, Janet." Carrie tucked the candy and gum into her purse, and then she and Austin said goodbye and walked out.

Debbie began pulling the leftover pastries out of the display case. "What was that about?"

Debbie had gotten acquainted with Carrie and Austin at church, but she probably didn't know Tyler. She had moved back to Dennison just over a year ago, when Tyler's success and subsequent fall from stardom wasn't news anymore.

"Their son, Tyler, is a baseball star, but since he had an injury and lost his scholarship, he's been having a hard time and getting into some trouble. He had a bad car accident a few weeks ago. Ian told me about it and said Tyler was lucky to be alive. I got the impression that alcohol was involved, though of course Ian didn't come out and say that."

"I'm glad he's okay," Debbie said. "No one else was hurt?"

"No, thankfully," Janet said. She locked the door then cleaned the last table. "In any case, he seems to be recovering from his knee surgery and getting back into baseball, so maybe he'll do better soon."

"Let's hope so." Debbie put the leftover pastries away, and together they finished cleaning the dining room. "See you bright and early," she said as they walked out to the parking lot.

"Enjoy your afternoon." Janet headed to her car and drove through the charming streets of Dennison.

The small town was pretty in all seasons, but in July the roses and hydrangeas were in full bloom, the leafy green oaks and plane trees shaded the streets, and the whole town seemed to burst with life and excitement. The downtown area was busy this afternoon, no doubt due to the people in town for the festival. It was going to be a busy week.

Janet swung by the grocery store on her way home. Once she got home and had unpacked everything in her kitchen, she put together a cold sesame noodle salad she planned to take to church that night. Pastor Nick was leading a Bible study on the book of Ruth, and everyone was encouraged to bring a dish to share. Janet looked forward to the lesson.

Ian came home from the police station in time for them to drive to the church together, and they enjoyed the potluck dinner and fellowship before Pastor Nick started explaining about the culture and history of the Israelites in the time of Ruth. By the time they were heading home, Janet was pleasantly full and sleepily mulling over the fascinating discussion. She relaxed in the passenger seat while Ian drove through the quiet streets.

She didn't really register the first siren. She vaguely heard the low whining sound but didn't think anything of it until Ian's phone rang. Janet glanced down at the phone resting on the console between their seats. *Mike Gleason*, it said on the screen. The head of the fire department. If he was calling Ian after work hours, it was probably important.

"It's the fire chief," she said. "Do you want me to answer it?"

"Sure," Ian said, nodding. "Thanks."

"Hi, Mike, this is Janet," she said. "Ian is driving."

"Hi, Janet." Mike Gleason was originally from Boston and had a thick accent, despite having spent the past several decades in Ohio. "Can you relay a message to him? Something big has come up."

A second siren came screaming up behind them, and Ian pulled over to the side of the road to let the oncoming fire truck pass.

"Sure. Where do you need him?" she asked over the noise. Ian was the chief of police for the small town of Dennison, and she was used to him being summoned to anything major that happened in town.

"Over at the warehouse on Stillwater. There's a fire."

Janet passed the message on to Ian.

"Tell him I'm on my way," Ian said. He followed the fire truck.

"He's on his way," Janet said into the phone. "We'll be there soon."

"Great. Thanks." The line went dead. Janet's first thought was that someone had been shooting off leftover fireworks and had sparked a fire. But she could see by the set of Ian's mouth that he was concerned.

"Are you familiar with this warehouse?" Janet vaguely knew where the row of warehouses was, on an industrial street on the outskirts of town.

"That's a municipal storage facility," Ian said. He pressed his foot down on the gas pedal. They were definitely over the speed limit, but the police chief wasn't likely to get a speeding ticket while responding to an emergency. "Lots of different departments store things there. The police department uses it to store crime-scene evidence."

"Does that mean—"

"It's where we store the evidence for all the crimes that have been committed in our area and for cases that are awaiting trial," Ian said grimly. "If it's on fire, that's a very bad thing."

A NOTE FROM the EDITORS

We hope you enjoyed another exciting volume in the Whistle Stop Café Mysteries series, published by Guideposts. For over seventy-five years, Guideposts, a nonprofit organization, has been driven by a vision of a world filled with hope. We aspire to be the voice of a trusted friend, a friend who makes you feel more hopeful and connected.

By making a purchase from Guideposts, you join our community in touching millions of lives, inspiring them to believe that all things are possible through faith, hope, and prayer. Your continued support allows us to provide uplifting resources to those in need. Whether through our communities, websites, apps, or publications, we inspire our audiences, bring them together, and comfort, uplift, entertain, and guide them. Visit us at guideposts.org to learn more.

We would love to hear from you. Write us at Guideposts, P.O. Box 5815, Harlan, Iowa 51593 or call us at (800) 932-2145. Did you love *Down Forget-Me-Not Lane*? Leave a review for this product on guideposts.org/shop. Your feedback helps others in our community find relevant products.

Find inspiration, find faith, find Guideposts.

Shop our best sellers and favorites at
guideposts.org/shop

Or scan the QR code to go directly to our Shop